UNSCREWED

UNSCREWED

THE CONSUMER'S GUIDE TO GETTING WHAT YOU PAID FOR

RON BURLEY

TEN SPEED PRESS
Berkeley | Toronto

Disclaimer: The information contained in this book is based on the experience and research of the author. The publisher and author are not responsible for any adverse consequences resulting from the use of any of the suggestions or procedures discussed.

Ten Speed Press
Box 7123
Berkeley, California 94707
www.tenspeed.com

Distributed in Australia by Simon and Schuster Australia, in Canada by Ten Speed Press Canada, in New Zealand by Southern Publishers Group, in South Africa by Real Books, and in the United Kingdom and Europe by Publishers Group UK.

Cover design by Ed Anderson
Interior design by Michael Cutter
Front cover photo by Steve Cole/Photodisc Green/Getty Images

Library of Congress Cataloging-in-Publication Data

Burley, Ron.
Unscrewed : the consumer's guide to getting what you paid for / Ron Burley.
       p. cm.
Summary: "A practical guide to getting what you paid for from uncaring, unscrupulous, and unavailable companies, including the government, through the creative and legal use of technology"—Provided by publisher.
Includes index.
ISBN-13: 978-1-58008-762-9
ISBN-10: 1-58008-762-0
1. Consumer protection—United States. 2. Fraud—United States. I. Title.
 HC110.C63B79 2006
 381.3'40973—dc22
                              2006011424

Printed in the United States of America
First printing, 2006

1 2 3 4 5 6 7 8 9 10—10 09 08 07 06

FOR HALI

CONTENTS

ACKNOWLEDGMENTS

The creation of this book was sparked by my brother, John, and my wonderful agent, Cathy Fowler, who asked, "What else have you been working on?"

Although the final product is my own, I must acknowledge inspiration from wonderfully intelligent conversations with Robert Kiyosaki, Keith Cunningham, Tom Gentry, Tony Cassara, and John McCanns.

The final product is the result of fine-tuning by a collection of readers and critique partners, including Larry Deckman, Coni Tarquini, Jerry Jump, and Sloan Heermance.

I would never have attempted the project without the encouragement of fellow authors and friends Elizabeth Engstrom-Cratty, Karen Joy Fowler, and Nancy Holder.

Finally, thank you, Mike Palmer, for telling me to stop going to conferences and just go home and write the book.

INTRODUCTION: WHY YOU NEED THIS BOOK

Every four seconds, an unsuspecting American consumer is bamboozled, betrayed, cheated, conned, deceived, defrauded, double-crossed, duped, fleeced, fooled, hoaxed, hoodwinked, lied to, misinformed, misled, phished, ripped off, robbed, scammed, shafted, stung, swindled, taken in, or tricked— more than seven million customers taken advantage of every year by an unscrupulous, uncaring, or unavailable company, corporation, or creep.

Any way you look at it, that's a lot of people getting screwed out of a lot of money. Of course, I'm not telling you anything new. If you hadn't experienced it for yourself, you probably wouldn't be reading this book. The harsh reality is that most of us have been victimized more than a few times.

This is no "Write them a nice letter and see whether they'll be nice back" kind of how-to book. This is a take-charge, "I'm going to get my money back" book for people who are tired of getting screwed!

That said, *Unscrewed: The Consumer's Guide to Getting What You Paid For* is *not* a guide to war or a revenge manual. It does not recommend personal attacks or destructive methods. At no time are you going to yell, throw a tantrum, or threaten bodily harm. The techniques are all legal and our goal is to level the playing field by creating a simple, obvious business equation that will result in the obstinate company doing the right thing—giving you what you are fairly due.

The core premise of the Unscrewed Solution is this: You must be in the right. You must be the one who has been wronged. It will not work if you are trying to get more than you deserve or put one over on a company that has done you no wrong. The strategies and tactics outlined in this book depend on the certain knowledge that you, the customer, have been mistreated by the company. In fact, if you were to attempt a "shakedown" of a company using these techniques, you just might end up in jail for fraud, theft, or harassment.

At the least, a company might have a good civil case against you for loss-of-business damages.

Everything in this book is based on personal, real-life experiences. No matter how implausible or incredible they may seem, the Unscrewed True Stories really happened. For legal reasons, and because I don't want someone's angry mother showing up on my doorstep, the names of most of the individuals and companies mentioned in the stories have been changed.

AN UNSCREWED HISTORY

In this book, the word *Unscrewed* refers to small vises that medieval torturers used to crush the thumbs of their victims. They would twist the vise screw into the top of the finger. Turn by turn, a steel pin would be driven farther and farther into the top of the fingernail, eventually piercing it, and creating excruciating pain. (This is the kind of pain that you experience when on voice mail hold for thirty minutes, listening to that inane music.) You become Unscrewed when you remove this diminutive diabolical device.

How you use the information provided in this book is entirely up to you. Neither the author nor the publisher can take credit or blame for how things turn out in your own efforts. However, if you use the techniques according to the Unscrewed Plan, you will have the ability to win satisfaction in virtually any situation without going to court—or to jail.

In the first three chapters of this book, you'll learn why you're getting screwed, and by whom. If you're getting screwed right now and need instant help, skip ahead to chapter 4, The Unscrewed Solution: The Five Ps. You can come back later and learn the reasons behind your pain.

The fact that there are so many names for getting screwed reminds me that the Inuit tribes of the Arctic have more than two dozen synonyms for *snow*. Their numerous names for the white stuff come from the fact that it is a familiar part of their daily lives. What does it mean for us that we've got as many names for being cheated as the Inuit have for snow? It means that *we* are more familiar with being taken advantage of than we should be.

Why are we so beleaguered?

Not all companies are crooked, but some are.

Not all megacorporations are disinterested in the individual consumer, but that is the case with many.

Not all problems can be blamed on a free enterprise system that promotes an atmosphere of "Make the sale at any cost," though some can.

All of these are factors, but they are still only part of the customer disservice equation. There are several other significant reasons why we're being victimized more now than before.

First of all, the number of businesses that we deal with on a daily basis has grown exponentially. A hundred years ago, the average household dealt with only a few companies on a regular basis: the local market, the blacksmith, a seed company, and maybe a doctor or vet. Most important, these were almost exclusively "local" companies with an interest in the community. On the other hand, think of all the companies, vendors, and institutions you deal with today:

Alarm Company	Cell Phone Company
Insurance Company	Real Estate Agent
Appliance Dealer	Clubs (Business and Civic)
Internet Provider	Schools
Auto Manufacturer	Credit Card Company
Lawyer	Supermarket
Auto Mechanic	Doctor
Mortgage Company	Ticket Outlet
Bank	Gas Station
Online Vendors and Services	Travel Agent
Cable Provider	Health Club
Phone Company	Utility Company

That's not even a complete list. I know you can think of more.

All those personal business relationships mean that you have that many more opportunities for mistakes, misunderstandings, and mischief. The mathematical probabilities favor it. Thankfully, given the chance, nine out of ten companies will do the right thing. But imagine, if every one of the two dozen companies you deal with commits just one mistake or misdeed per year, then you would be dealing with a situation that needs to be Unscrewed about every two weeks.

The second reason that consumers are being victimized more often is that the bottom-line economic pressures on companies are greater now than ever before. Globalization, online shopping, and mega-outlets have changed the retail business landscape. As second-world and third-world nations enter the multinational economy, companies are facing a greater number of competitors than ever before. In a do-or-die battle to cut costs, many companies have slashed Customer Service Departments, replaced them with technological obstructions, and created customer service policies that are actually a disservice to their customers.

The third reason is that today, unlike a century ago, many of the businesses you deal with are not local. Companies that used to be based in your community—your phone company, cable company, mortgage company, and even dry cleaner—are now often part of a national chain, removing any sense of loyalty to your community.

Finally, your day is already full, and your ability to get timely satisfaction for a problem is being constantly eroded. It's at the point where you, like many consumers, just decide it isn't worth it—leaving millions of dollars per year in the hands of corporations and individuals that didn't earn it. To you, it's a loss. They call it "unearned profit."

In short, you're not imagining that you're getting screwed more often. You are!

WHY I WROTE THIS BOOK

During my dozen years' reporting for television and radio, I often heard from people about how they were either being taken advantage of or not being listened to by inscrutable companies. The complaints ranged from small—a call on their telephone bill they knew they hadn't made—to large—a mortgage company threatening foreclosure even though the mortgage check had cleared the bank.

I learned that in this era, the traditional ways of getting companies to listen to complaints—calling or writing—frequently don't work. Even threats of going to court or to the state attorney general are often ignored. Why? Because the decision makers in those companies know that you're not really going to do it, particularly over a couple of hundred dollars, sloppy service, or a botched paint job. Your adversaries are counting on the fact that those options are too expensive, time-consuming, and complex for most of us.

After I left journalism and started several businesses of my own, I was amazed by the number of companies I dealt with that failed to fulfill their promises or contractual obligations. When I challenged them, I was often ignored, brushed off, or in some other manner told to go away. Even threatening to withhold my business didn't faze the big guys: the credit card company, phone company, and bank.

I went through the normal routines of writing letters, phoning, cajoling, being the nice guy, being the bad guy, pleading for mercy, and threatening them with court—almost always to no effect. I couldn't understand why companies would treat me as if they didn't care whether I ever came back. The cliché was, "The customer is always right." That maxim was clearly out of date.

There had to be a better way to get their attention. I started to research customer service warranties and guarantees. I studied the historical relationship between businesses and their customers. I talked with customer service insiders to get some insight into why things are the way they are today, as compared with years gone by. Those investigations, and one incident in particular that I share later in this introduction, led me to develop The Unscrewed Solution.

In this book, you will learn a set of sometimes unorthodox, but very effective, methods for dealing with intractable
companies, corporations, or crooks. Most of them can be
accomplished in an afternoon, some in just minutes.

The Unscrewed Solution has nothing to do with mailing
letters, begging for mercy, or going to court. I often learned
the hard way—through failure—what not to do. I share those
stories in later chapters. I've been able to refine the techniques
with the selection of just the right words, manner, and message—so that I am now pleased to say that it has been several
years since I've lost a consumer battle.

My promise to you is that if you follow the plan, you will
walk away from the great majority of situations satisfied, where
otherwise you might have been taken advantage of or ignored.

As I've already said, more than what I heard from other
consumers or learned from my own unfortunate experiences
inspired this book. In particular, there was one personal
episode in the early 1990s that opened my eyes to a simple
principle that would eventually become the foundation of
The Unscrewed Solution.

UNSCREWED TRUE STORY

The Unscrupulous Car Dealer

When I was a young reporter, earning just enough to get
by in the high-rent lifestyle of Honolulu, I had finally managed to scrape together the down payment on a new car.
I got up one Saturday morning and headed out to Auto
Row. I shopped around and found a very functional four-
door sedan. Happy as a Kaneohe clam, I drove away in my
new car an hour or so later. It was practical and ran well.

However, two days after I bought the car, I noticed an
ad in the local newspaper. (It was a few days old because
I'd been busy.) In the ad, the dealership where I had
bought my car was advertising a discount of $1,500 for

any car purchased over the weekend. I'd been able to get the guy to take off $300 and toss in some floor mats, but it looked as though he'd forgotten to mention the advertised special.

I called up the dealership. The sales manager told me, "There's nothing we can do. The contract is signed and the loan approved. I wish we could, but we just can't."

I replied, "What do you mean? You advertised the special. The sales representative should have told me about it! It's just not fair."

"That's our policy. I'm sorry."

"It's a bad policy," I said, for lack of any other words, and hung up the phone.

I was livid. I'd just been screwed out of $1,200, less the cost of a couple of floor mats.

Something had to be done.

I steamed and fumed for several hours. I thought I'd take them to court, but wasn't sure how, and wasn't really sure whether I had a case. I wanted to call some government agency in charge of fairness in advertising, but I wasn't sure that the dealer was required to tell me about the ad. The problem was, although the situation was patently unfair, it probably wasn't illegal. I paced my small apartment for another hour or two until I hit upon an idea. Because money was apparently the only thing that really mattered, I would simply make it more expensive to ignore me than to give me what I deserved.

I sat down at my computer and typed out a few words in large letters. Then I printed up a couple dozen copies of my creation, stuck them in a manila folder, and drove to the dealership. It had been only forty-eight hours since I purchased my new car, but as soon as I drove onto the lot, I could tell that the word had been spread that I was a "problem" customer.

Instead of the cheery salesperson meeting me at the glass double doors, the sales manager appeared and said tersely, "Mr. Burley, as I told you on the phone, there's nothing we can do. All the paperwork has been sent in."

I stood my ground, looked him in the eye, and asked if we could go to his office. He stared back quizzically, but he agreed to my request. We walked to his office. He sat down behind his chipped cherry veneer desk, and I took a chair on the other side.

"Mr. Smith," I said, "I'm here to ask you one last time to do what is right. You advertised the $1,500 discount, and I should have received it. Nowhere in the advertisement did it say that I had to bring in a coupon or even mention the ad. Therefore, you owe me $1,200."

"That's not the way we see it at Akamai Motors. As I said on the phone, it's our internal policy not to revise contracts after they've been signed." He looked bored.

"Mr. Smith," I replied, "your internal policy doesn't interest me. We are talking about what is right, and speaking of rights, I am prepared to exercise mine."

Mr. Smith's eyebrows rose, making him look remarkably like the cartoon dog Scooby-Doo. "What do you mean by that? Are you going to take us to court? If that's what you're saying, then this discussion has to stop right here."

"No, I'm not talking about court. I'm talking about the First Amendment."

He gave me another Scooby-Doo look.

"I'm still confused."

I put the manila folder in the center of the desk so that the pages would be facing him. I opened it to reveal a flyer, printed in red and black.

"What do you intend to do with those?" he asked. I had his attention now.

"Mr. Smith," I said coolly, even though my hands were sweaty and shaking, "at this point, it doesn't really matter to me whether I get my money back or not. I am going to exercise my First Amendment right to stand on that public sidewalk in front of your dealership. I'll hand one of these flyers to anybody walking onto your lot. I'll be carrying a picket sign with the same message."

Mr. Smith was speechless. The Scooby-Doo look was gone. He looked more like a frightened rabbit.

AKAMAI MOTORS LIES TO ITS CUSTOMERS!

They advertised a car at one price and then sold it to me for $1,200 more. For details, please call Ron Burley at 808-555-5555.

I continued, "I'll bet that, in just a handful of Saturdays, I can convince a couple of dozen people to shop elsewhere. It could end up that, by not paying me what's due me, you lose ten times that much in future business. It won't put any cash in my pocket, but I'll feel a lot better about things. What do you think?"

Mr. Smith pushed back from the desk. "Give me just a minute," he said. He stood up and left the room. I sat in his office, reading the plaques on the wall, until he returned. He sat down behind the desk and smiled at me.

"Ron, I was wrong. I double-checked with our general manager, and he says that we should have honored the advertisement all along, whether you knew about it or not. Please accept my apology for the misunderstanding. I just try to follow policy, and sometimes the wires get crossed."

I smiled back. "Thank you, Doug. I'm glad we straightened that out. When can I get my check?"

"Bookkeeping is taking care of it right now, if you can wait a few minutes."

"Certainly," I said. I walked out of the dealership ten minutes later, holding a check for $1,200. I had left the flyers on Doug's desk.

Driving to the bank to deposit the check, I thought, *No letter writing. No court threats. I have a check and didn't even have to pass out my flyers. There could be something to this approach!*

THE PROBLEM

THE EROSION OF CONSUMER CLOUT

I loved Democrat Howard Dean's war cry in the presidential campaign of 2004. He finished each speech by cheering, "You've got the power! You've got the power! *You've got the power!*" As much as I liked the message, I couldn't help thinking that most consumers feel as though they've been losing "the power." It's no wonder they feel that way: they have.

The erosion of consumer clout is happening simultaneously in many quarters. National statistics prove it. Since 1990, consumer complaints are up more than 30 percent—while the best information available about complaint resolution tells us that fewer than 1 percent ever get resolved to the customer's satisfaction. A lot of people are taking it on the chin.

Here are some of the numbers:

- In 2004, more than 2 million consumer complaints were filed with the Federal Trade Commission (FTC). Only 21,940 of them were investigated. Just over 2,000 cases, covering just under 25,000 of the complainants, were decided in their favor.
- The Consumer Product Safety Commission received 1.9 million reports from consumers in 2004. Fewer than 5,000 resulted in legal action.
- In 2003, more than 1.7 million cases of identity theft were reported to the FTC. Identity theft often results in

a multitude of problems for the victim, who is expected to clean up the mess. Adding insult to injury, the theft is often the result of a company's lax security.

- Consumers filed more than 1.5 million complaints with the Better Business Bureaus of America (BBB) in 2004. When a complaint is filed, the BBB sends a letter to the company. However, it has no legal power or enforcement ability. Companies can simply ignore the complaint. The BBB doesn't publish a comprehensive report of offending companies. If you ask, they will tell you only the number of documented complaints filed against a specific company. Even that number is not an accurate record. A company can often have a complaint removed from the BBB files by simply writing a one-sided letter of explanation.

SUCK YOU IN, SPIT YOU OUT

These numbers reflect only reported incidents. Customer satisfaction surveys from several industries indicate that at least half of victimized consumers never file a complaint. The data indicate that many of these dissatisfied customers first try to have a problem solved by a company's customer service department. When that fails, rather than reporting the problem, they simply take their business elsewhere.

In the past, customer retention was the name of the game for successful businesses. Building "brand loyalty" among consumers was the goal. It was considered bad business to have a high "churn" percentage—meaning that a company was losing a significant portion of their customer base at the same time that they were attempting to attract new customers. That's changed. Today, churn is an accepted part of many business models.

In the cell phone industry, for example, the churn rate averages an amazing 30 percent per year. This means that nearly one-third of cell phone customers are so dissatisfied with their service every year that they choose to change carriers—and these are successful companies! More astonishing is that these statistics are for years when it meant that cell phone users would have to change their phone numbers when they changed providers. That's a big hassle, and a strong indication of how frustrated the "churned" customers must be.

This is certainly not true for all companies or industries. Many companies have worked hard to improve customer service and reward brand loyalty. The U.S. automobile industry has made great strides in the past decade in reported levels of customer satisfaction. Yet despite those gains by the manufacturers, auto *dealers* rank among the companies most complained about to the Federal Trade Commission.

The acceptance of churn is why you keep getting more and more credit card solicitations in your mailbox but can't get a live person from your current company on the phone. It's why every bank in the country is trying to get you to refinance your home, but your own bank is cutting back on services and increasing fees. The acceptance of churn means that many businesses have decided that it is less expensive to attract new customers than it is to take care of old ones. In short, for many industries, the individual customer has become disposable.

TECHNOLOGY TO THE RESCUE
Even companies that don't have a high churn rate are looking to cut costs and improve profit margins. In the 1990s, the buzzword for business was *service*. Every company was touting its high level of customer satisfaction and service. After the crash of 2000 and the subsequent recession, trimming the bottom line became more important than boosting satisfaction numbers. Laying off customer service people, who didn't really add to sales numbers, was a quick and easy cost reduction. They were often replaced with voice mail, e-mail, or Internet customer service options that cost far less.

Companies presented these "innovations" as evidence of their attempts to become more responsive to their customers. However, anyone who's ever battled his or her way through a half-dozen levels of voice mail, only to realize that there's no way to talk with a live person, can tell you that this is

Orwellian doublespeak. The voice mail service and Internet service options really present greater obstacles to customers seeking solutions.

Other companies took a different strategy, which provided just as much bad news for consumers. Companies that couldn't entirely replace their flesh-and-blood service representatives with technological substitutes found other ways to cut customer service costs.

Between 2000 and 2005, more than half the customer service call centers based in the United States were "offshored." Companies subcontracted their customer service needs to other companies, frequently in other countries. The largest call centers in the world are now in India and Israel. So when you finally do reach a customer service representative for Company X, that person might actually work for Company Z. Because this customer service representative is not an employee of Company X, he or she might be equipped with only a scripted set of limited solutions, none of which fits your problem.

Even when you get through to a person who works for Company X, you might be in for a surprise. At the same time that they were limiting your customer service options, companies were limiting their liability in terms of what they were legally required to provide in terms of customer care, technical support, and product warranties.

CLICKING AWAY YOUR RIGHTS

Many companies, particularly software and online service vendors, have you electronically sign an "end user license agreement," or EULA, before you can use or gain access to their products. You've probably just clicked right through it as you installed a new software program. You are usually told to read a long legal document describing the limitations of a product or service before you select an on-screen button labeled, "I Agree." Most people do not realize that with that simple click, they have entered into a binding contract with the company and have agreed to all the terms of that contract.

EULAs started out as legal protections against piracy or theft of intellectual property. The legal scouts working for the companies soon realized that they could make additional use of the EULA: they inserted a broad range of protections for the company and removed many consumer rights. Early on, a number of consumer advocates challenged the use of EULAs, but courts have repeatedly upheld the right of companies to use them.

Even though most of us have been faced with EULAs, it's fair to say that few of us have ever actually read one. It's not that we're lazy. We're just trusting. We assume the agreements are written fairly and provide an appropriate means for settling disputes. In fact, many EULAs grant the company sole discretion to decide when and how to deal with customer issues.

The most egregious and absurd of the stipulations in many EULAs is the ability of the software company to charge to fix a product that you've already paid for. The company might have the tact to call this repair an upgrade. But in the end, you pay twice for the same product. More than one software industry critic has quipped that "requiring a customer to pay for a software fix is the equivalent of asking someone to pay extra for tires when he buys a new car."

THE GLOBAL CORNER STORE

While many companies are finding ways to limit their customer service costs, they are simultaneously distancing themselves from our communities and daily lives. National and international chains have bought up smaller operations to create megacorporations, losing the important community connections that made them responsive to their customers. Your local hardware store is gone—replaced by a Home Depot outlet. These days, even a business that looks local might not be. You're often dealing with a franchise location of a national company. Unfortunately for you, franchisees often don't have much wiggle room as far as customer satisfaction policies go, and the national company has little interest in dealing with you as an individual.

These massive retailers enter markets and push out smaller competitors. In 1999, for the first time in our nation's commercial history, nationally owned or franchise retail businesses outnumbered locally owned businesses.

Just a few decades ago, only the largest corporations—oil, auto, and mining companies—were multinational. That is changing. Many more historically U.S. companies, in a variety of industries, from telecommunications to drug manufacturing, are now multinational or even completely foreign-owned.

The third-largest U.S. automaker is now a German company: Mercedes purchased Chrysler to form Daimler Chrysler. IBM laptops are no longer made by IBM: the Lenovo Group of the People's Republic of China purchased that division of Big Blue in 2004. Fox Television and scores of U.S. newspapers and television stations are owned by Australian native Rupert Murdoch, who is now a naturalized U.S. citizen, primarily for the purpose of buying even more of our media infrastructure. Even the quintessential rags-to-riches American success story, Standard Oil—founded by John D. Rockefeller—is now a wholly owned subsidiary of British Petroleum.

Despite all of the bad news about the erosion of customer clout, most companies still provide adequate levels of customer service. In this book, we're concerned with the ones that don't.

This does not include a person or company that commits criminal fraud or theft. If that's the case, your first call should be to the local district attorney, and you should probably give up hope of ever getting your money back. The only good news is that, in some rare cases, you may have a legitimate claim to file with your insurance company.

For all the reasons discussed in this chapter, the U.S. consumer has lost, and will continue to lose, bargaining power in the marketplace. We've become disposable commodities: it's less expensive to replace us than to please us. It's less trouble to ignore us than to listen to us, and less effort to deny a problem than to solve it.

That is the situation we must change, and that is exactly what The Unscrewed Solution is designed to do.

UNSCREWED TRUE STORY
The Telephone Installation Nightmare

A few years ago, shortly after I first began giving Unscrewed seminars, my friend Jack called me in a panic. He had just moved into a new house and set up his home office.

Jack ran an Internet sales company from his home and needed to stay in constant communication with his customers, distant employees, and vendors. He also maintained the company web site, which was hosted off-site. Needless to say, it was crucial that he have quality phone service and a reliable connection to the Internet.

Jack had worked with his phone company for a couple of months before the move, to make sure that the transition from the old location to the new location would go smoothly. He had arranged for a new eight-pair cable to be buried and connected at his new house. That one cable would carry all phone and Internet communications. The upgrade had cost Jack more than $1,000, but he considered it worth it to ensure that things went well on moving day.

Because he had wanted to make sure that there would be no gap in telephone or Internet service, he was very concerned about the timing of the move. The phone company representative told him, "No problem. Don't worry. Trust me. We're on top of it." He repeatedly promised that the lines would be transferred without missing a beat.

Moving day was a Monday, but Jack got a head start. Over the weekend, he moved all the office furniture and even plugged the phones into the jacks. Based on what the phone company representative had told him, sometime between 8:00 and 8:30 on Monday morning, the lines would magically start working.

A little after 8:00 on Monday, Jack began scanning the morning paper and nervously checking for a dial tone every few minutes. When 8:45 had come and gone, and he still didn't hear that comforting tone when he picked up the receiver, Jack used his cell phone to call the representative. Instead of the man Jack had been talking to for many weeks, a woman answered. "I'm sorry, he's no longer with the company," she said. "Maybe I can help you. Are you currently a customer? Is this a residential or business service?"

It was 9:00 a.m. on the first business day in his new location. Jack was talking with an agent of the phone company who didn't even know that he was a customer. Dumbfounded, Jack gave her the whole story: order numbers, phone line codes, and installation dates.

"Have the lines been commissioned?"

"What do you mean, 'commissioned'? Do you mean installed?" Jack was livid. "Yes, then. But all I really want to know is when my phones will work!"

"It may take a while, sir," she replied. "We have procedures that we must follow."

"Oh, come on! I've got a business to run!" he shouted.

"I'm sorry, sir. I can't continue this conversation if you're going to speak to me in that way," replied the agent.

"I'm not speaking to you in any 'way.' But you don't get it. I'm losing business because your company dropped the ball. I need this taken care of now! What are you going to do about it?" Jack waited for a response: all he got was a click, silence, and then a dial tone.

He tried calling back, but the line was busy. He called the phone company's main service number. They gave him a "trouble code" and told him that his problem would be taken care of within three business days. He repeated his story that the original agent had promised that the lines would be up that morning. He let them know that he would be losing business and customers every minute that the lines weren't working.

"We take all trouble calls in the order in which they're received," said the repair agent.

"But I've been dealing with you for months on this. I doubt anybody is in line ahead of me," Jack retorted.

"I'm sorry, but that's our policy."

"It's a bad policy," Jack said, and pushed the "END" button on his cell phone.

Something had to be done.

That was when Jack called me and told me the story. We lived near each other. I told him to gather up all of the paperwork on the phone project and bring it to my office. I'd let him use my phone and Internet connection until we got his situation…Unscrewed.

Jack arrived fifteen minutes later—looking quite frazzled—with notes in hand. He'd done a couple of things right: he'd kept track of all the order numbers and had notes on several of the conversations. Unfortunately, he'd not gotten the name of the representative who'd hung up on him.

The situation was urgent. Jack was losing orders by the minute. Because he'd already tried to fix things the nice way and failed, I suggested that we go straight to the top with a technique I call Faxing for Dollars. (A complete description of this technique is in chapter 13.)

Most corporations are secretive about their internal fax numbers. They don't want to receive lots of junk faxes and they prefer that customers deal with the Customer Service Department. However, if you know where and how to look, you can usually find ways around their veil of secrecy.

Corporations are required by law to file all kinds of disclosure documents. They are also required to disclose publicly certain correspondence. They also like to toot their own horn in press releases and encourage investment through various communications.

After just a few minutes of cruising the Internet, I was able to locate several documents that contained unpublished fax numbers for the phone company executives, including the company president, chair, vice president of customer relations, and the national sales manager.

With that information in hand, Jack and I drafted a brief letter stating the facts of the case, his loss of business, and how he could be contacted. The letter closed with the line, "I promise that you will see me at every Public Utility Commission meeting for the next ten years, telling my story of how your screwup cost me thousands of dollars in lost business, unless this problem is taken care of today. Best regards, Jack."

"What do we do now?" asked my friend.

"Just watch," I said. I logged onto an Internet fax service, uploaded the letter, and typed in the four numbers I'd found. I pasted them into the address box again and again and again—until each number was listed fifty times. I glanced at the clock. It read 10:05 a.m. I clicked the send button.

"This shouldn't take long," I said.

As I poured us each a cup of coffee, I imagined those fax machines, far away, spewing out our letter, dozens and dozens of times. I visualized the faces of the administrative assistants as they realized that the same letter kept coming and coming and coming. I imagined the national sales manager, waiting for contracts and reports to flow from his fax machine, standing mute as our letter filled the tray instead.

At 10:23, my business phone rang. I answered it. "It's for you," I said, looking at Jack. "It's the phone company's vice president of customer relations." One of the faxes made it through the corporate bastions and quickly landed on her desk.

Jack took the phone. He listened, mumbling a few "uh-huhs" and a "thank you." Then he hung up.

"So what's going on?" I asked.

"She promised they'd have a technician at my house within the hour."

"Great!" I responded. "That's not all," Jack said. "She apologized for the trouble, and said they're going to credit me for the cost of the installation, including the new lines."

So Jack got his phones working. For less than two hours of grief, he also ended up with a $1,000 credit from the phone company. Not bad for a morning's work.

THE TRUTH ABOUT CUSTOMER SERVICE

I t seems illogical, but these days, the primary goal of many corporate Customer Service Departments is *not* to provide service to the customer.

When you call Customer Service, or Customer Support, or the Quality Assurance Department—the name doesn't matter—you rightfully expect to get someone on the line who will help solve a problem you have with that company's product or service. On the surface, it appears that the Customer Service Department's role in the business-customer relationship is to make sure that customers are satisfied with the company's product or service. But if we take a look at what they do, rather than what they say, we find that just beneath the glossy veneer, the reality is far different.

In an ideal world, customer service representatives would give you exactly what you deserve as soon as they promptly answered the phone, or as soon as you walked up to the desk. They would listen carefully to your problem and respond to your questions with thoughtful answers. Your product would be replaced or problem resolved as quickly as humanly possible, and you would receive a sincere apology. A few days to a week later, you would receive a follow-up call to make sure that everything was still to your liking.

Although some companies do provide that kind of stellar customer service, more often than not—and certainly more often than should happen—we are faced with the antiversion of that idyllic customer-company interaction.

As corporate budgets have tightened and churn has become an acceptable business model, Customer Service Departments have turned into "cost reduction" departments, where their primary job is to provide you something less than what you ask for, or rightly deserve. It is their job to improve the company's bottom line by reducing "customer service and support costs," which means that they are in the business of making sure they give you the lowest cost solution that will make you go away in the least amount of time.

Don't they care about keeping you as a customer? Not really. As an individual, you are insignificant in the overall business plan. Moreover, once you are identified as a customer who calls Customer Support, which costs them money, you are labeled an "unwanted problem customer." *It's cheaper to replace you than to take care of you.*

The cell phone industry again provides one of the best examples of this customer service devolution. The average call to the Customer Service Department of a cell phone company costs $20; this includes employee time, capital costs or contract costs, and, of course, the cost of the product or refund they end up providing. Statistically, customers who call Customer Service will likely call again, costing the company even more. On the other hand, new customers can be hooked by an average of only $4 in marketing costs. For the amount of money it would cost to satisfy your complaint, the company could recruit five new customers. For anyone familiar with the cold, calculating world of business accounting, it makes much more sense to send you packing than to try to make you happy.

It's easy to see why many businesses have little interest in retaining you as a customer or working to keep your repeat business. The cost reduction model of customer service requires that the representatives do whatever they can to minimize the cost of correcting their company's failing. It is an adversarial relationship, where they begin the conversation with the goal of making sure you don't get everything you deserve. If you insist on fair treatment, you are all but encouraged to take your business elsewhere.

For most of us who grew up with the idea that "the customer is always right," this warped neo-reality of the customer service industry seems like something out of *Alice in Wonderland*.

Many retails chains have decided that they can eliminate their customer service costs completely if they never have to deal with you at all. They have hammered out relationships with suppliers that mean that the stores don't have to deal with damaged or faulty merchandise.

Here's how they've sidestepped any responsibility to take care of you. If the new toaster you purchased fails to work an hour after you take it out of the box, you rightfully expect that you should be able to return it immediately to the store where you bought it, have it replaced, and possibly even have the new one tested to make sure that it works properly.

In the "no backs" customer service model, you'll discover that, once you've made your purchase, fine print policies absolve the retailer of any responsibility in providing repair or replacement of a faulty product. Inside the box, you'll find a warranty card that says, "Do Not Return Faulty or Damaged Merchandise to the Store." You are directed to return defective products to a distant manufacturer or distributor.

Many people, when faced with the "no backs" warranty, attempt to get a refund, in lieu of the replacement. However, if you've already revealed to the store that the product is faulty, your request is likely to be rejected. Not all is lost. There are several techniques you can use to get what you deserve in this situation. (We'll dive into the techniques themselves beginning in chapter 5.)

As we can see, the retailers have found a way to keep you from taking up their time and compromising their bottom line: they send you to the manufacturer. Meanwhile, manufacturers and distributors have developed anti–customer service practices of their own. They shield themselves behind an electronic barrier of Internet e-mail support or telephone voice mail.

Try the e-mail route and you might be fortunate enough to receive an automated response stating that they have

---

BUY AND SWITCH—EFFECTIVE, BUT NOT ETHICAL

A few years ago, an Unscrewed seminar attendee offered her solution to the "no backs" customer service scenario. She used what she called the Buy and Switch solution. She told the story of purchasing a new digital camera to take pictures at her daughter's wedding. After getting it home and inserting the batteries, she discovered that the tiny LCD view screen on the back of the camera didn't work. The warranty card warned her not to return it to the store, but rather, to ship it to a factory repair center in another state. The wedding was only two days away, so she couldn't wait. Instead, she went to a different branch of the same store and bought a second camera of the exact manufacture and model. After making sure that it worked fine, she packed up the first camera in the second camera's box and returned it to the store. "What a coincidence! My husband just told me that he already bought me one for my birthday next week." She was cheerfully given a refund, and was able to take some beautiful pictures at her daughter's wedding that weekend.

Although effective, there are some ethical problems with the Buy and Switch solution. First of all, the faulty camera will go back on the shelf and be sold to another unsuspecting customer. You may have Unscrewed yourself, but you've ended up "screwing" someone else. Meanwhile, the store and the manufacturer have avoided taking any responsibility for their poor customer service policies. Therefore, this is *not* a solution I recommend or endorse. We consumers need to find solutions that benefit us all, or else the circle of corporate victimization will never end.

received your message and will get back to you at some future time. Just as often, your e-mail inquiry disappears into the black hole of the Internet, and you never hear from the company at all.

If you try to reach them by telephone, you run into a voice mail labyrinth; your chances of making contact with a flesh-and-blood human being aren't good. When you finally do reach someone, that person may be a contract employee in a distant country who doesn't actually get a paycheck from the company you've done business with, whose answers are limited to the pages of a script, and whose ability to provide customer satisfaction is limited to, "I'm sorry: that's our policy."

Unfortunately, many of us give up when finally presented with that simple phrase, "It's our policy." But in the Unscrewed world, those are fighting words. In this world, "I'm sorry: that's our policy" is just the beginning of the interaction. It is the equivalent of throwing down the glove, drawing a line in the sand, or revving your engine at a stoplight.

I can't count the number of times that I've heard an employee spout that phrase, as if it were a magic wand that would somehow make me disappear. What those words really mean is that the company has put in place a "policy" designed to turn away customers who dare to ask for what they deserve. They create an adversarial relationship, where customers are forced to battle with the companies to whom they originally demonstrated loyalty by purchasing their products or services. We innocently entered into a financial relationship with them. We gave them money, representing our hard work, for a product or service that we trusted was of high quality from a reputable company. When the "quality" factor of the equation falls apart, we expect companies to stand behind the products and services they sell. When they fail to fulfill that part of the equation, we feel betrayed, cheated, and angry. Our initial response is to lash out at the first company representative we are able to contact. We threaten to take them to court, to tell all our friends, and to write letters to the editor. They don't care.

In the next story, a customer service insider tells us what happened at her company when the bubble burst.

UNSCREWED TRUE STORY

The Rise and Fall of Triple Time Software

In 2004, after a session of the Unscrewed seminar, I was approached by one of the attendees, Teri. She found me in the hotel corridor and asked if I'd like to have coffee with her. She thought I might be interested in hearing about her experiences as a five-year veteran of a software company Customer Service Department.

"Of course," I said. We found a quiet corner table in the hotel coffee shop, and Teri began telling me her story. She told me how she'd joined Triple Time Software's Customer Satisfaction Department within weeks of receiving a BA in marketing from a well-known Midwestern university. They recruited her at a job fair held at the school. Triple Time was just one of several dozen companies vying for the most talented of the new graduates.

For the first couple of years, she felt good about the job she was doing. "It was a great place to work," Teri said. "You felt that you were part of a team and that anything was possible. We were all sure that we were going to be the next Microsoft."

Triple Time's senior management preached a doctrine that quality customer support was integral to their future prosperity. The company provided monthly training on the use, care, and configuration of their products. They also trained the support team on how to deal with customer problems respectfully and quickly. The support team was constantly reminded that "a satisfied customer is our best advertising."

Triple Time's employees felt great about the company: it was riding the tech wave of the late 1990s. Many of them were already software millionaires, at least on paper—had they been able to cash in their stock options.

There were monthly brainstorming-and-pizza parties, where different departments would get together to share ideas on how they could improve products and customer service. The best ideas were rewarded with trips and cash bonuses.

The annual employee meeting was always held in the summer at a nice beachfront resort in Southern California. It was a golden time—for the company, for the employees, and for the customers. Unfortunately, it didn't last long.

In late 1999—when the bubble burst in the tech industry—Triple Time's stock price plummeted. At the same time, many long-time customers cut back on new purchases and updates. In a matter of months, Triple Time's financial picture went from bright to bird poop. Of course, they weren't alone in suffering financial hard times: many other tech companies just took down their signs and locked their doors.

"It happened so fast," Teri says. "It felt as though we went home for the weekend and everything was fine. Then we came back on Monday, and our dreams had turned to dust."

To survive the tough times near the end of the millennium, Triple Time management decide to cut operating costs wherever they could. The pizza parties disappeared; no one was in the mood to schmooze anyway. Who would want to talk about improving the products and service when they weren't sure they would be with the company long enough to pick up the next week's paycheck? The customer support training classes were canceled. Employees who left weren't replaced. Eventually, some layoffs were necessary. Finally, everyone in the company, including top management, took a 20 percent pay cut. Mere survival was the name of the game. Nothing was sacred; no job untouchable. Rewards were given to employees who came up with ideas for the company to reduce administrative, sales, and customer service costs. The atmosphere became hostile as employees tried to save their own jobs by figuring out how to eliminate someone else's position.

A year after the big crunch, Teri became head of a much smaller Customer Support Department. Of the original forty-five members of the team, only a dozen remained. From the customer's point of view, Triple Time's telephone tech support had turned into a voice mail marathon.

To get more immediate service, clients could opt to join a subscription customer support program for a hefty monthly fee. Customers who elected not to subscribe were left with the online support, but that provided answers only to known technical issues, and was updated only when someone in the Customer Support Department had the time to write up the new issues and post them online. "Which was like, never," Teri said. "We were stretched so thin that, in the end, even the subscription customers often waited an hour to get through."

She remembered getting a call one winter afternoon from a company that offered to handle their technical support for them. Contract technical support had been around for years, though it was generally considered a poor substitute for in-house operations. Not only would Universal Support Services (USS) not be in house, but they also wouldn't even be in the country. The USS customer support call center was in India. Despite the distance, USS claimed that they could process customer calls for less than 20 percent of the cost of Triple Time's own operation, and they promised better response times. It sounded too good to be true, but the USS client list included some of the top companies in the industry.

Teri's feelings were mixed: contracting USS to provide Triple Time's customer support would save a lot of money, but it would also mean that most of the remaining in-house support team would be laid off. Teri took it to top management, who decided to sign on with USS. Laid-off support staff were given generous severance packages. In the end, Teri was left with three employees and a contract with a company halfway around the world.

Sitting across the table from me in the hotel café, Teri was almost apologetic. "You have to understand: there really wasn't an alternative. From a cost standpoint, it made sense for there to be a single call center, instead of a dozen software companies each having one of its own."

"But could they really provide service?" I asked. "How much did they know about your products?"

She took a few breaths while forming her answer. "We provided USS with a database of all our issues and developed a decision tree," Teri said. "By talking the customer through a series of questions, they could solve 90 percent of the issues."

"What about the other 10 percent?"

Teri stirred a spoon in her half-empty cup. "We called them casualties."

"What do you mean?"

"If USS couldn't handle them," Teri paused and then continued, "then they were out of luck."

"Couldn't anyone at Triple Time handle the tough cases?"

"Well, that's kind of the point. We didn't want to. Most of us felt that the problems encountered by the tough customers were really of their own making. I mean, we knew our product worked fine, and that 99.9 percent of our clients were happy. So we just decided that the leftovers either had hardware problems, which had nothing to do with us, or were too…inexperienced…to figure out what they needed to do."

"You were going to say *stupid*."

"Yes," Teri replied apologetically. "But that was how we felt. Management calculated that it would cost us far more to work things out with those people than they could possibly be worth to the company."

"They were disposable."

Teri stared across the café at some distant point and then back at me.

"I haven't ever really thought of it that way," she said, now looking into the bottom of her coffee cup. "I suppose you're right, though. We really just didn't want to deal with them anymore. It was too much of a headache." She paused for a moment and then looked me in the eye as she said slowly, "We wanted them to go somewhere else. We wanted them to become somebody else's problem."

Something had to be done.

THE FAILURE OF CONVENTIONAL SOLUTIONS

ustomer complaints have been around since the first time a cave dweller traded a gazelle leg for a stone club, and later discovered a crack in the handle. Back then, the dispute was probably resolved quickly—most likely with the meat recipient emerging victorious. After all, he still had a club that worked.

Throughout the centuries, customer complaint scenarios evolved along with human society. As our agrarian economy gave way to the industrial revolution, which morphed into the information age, companies couldn't behave like the cave dweller and club complaining customers into submission. They had to deal with them. Eventually, companies became adept at providing only the minimum necessary to make complainers go away—or ignoring them completely.

Unsatisfied customers needed ways to get companies to listen to them, to provide satisfaction. Accepted methods for dealing with customer service problems were developed. Look on the shelves of today's bookstores, and you'll find that most consumer how-to manuals suggest one or more of the following traditional methods.

CONVENTIONAL SOLUTION NUMBER ONE: WRITE A LETTER

Once the first call to a Customer Service Department fails to meet our expectations, conventional wisdom tells us the best way to deal with the problem is to write a letter that will make our case, show how we are in the right, and demonstrate how we have been wronged by the company.

The biggest problem with letter writing is that it is so…slow. Most of us don't write letters these days, even if we can figure out what the current postage rate is and can find a stamp to put on the envelope.

So you write the letter, put it in the mailbox, and wait for a reply—which may never come. When it does, you're likely to receive a "Thank you for your inquiry. However, it's not our policy to…" letter that, in polite corporate language, tells you to go away and stop bugging them.

This exchange of letters could take weeks, even months. Most of us aren't willing to engage in that kind of tedious dialogue. And if you are, the odds are pretty good that during that time, the person you've been dealing with will have been fired, promoted, or transferred, and you'll have to start all over again with somebody new. "Are you a customer of ours?"

Some companies don't even bother to respond to your letter. They've learned that—statistically—the best response to a complaint letter is just to ignore it, toss it, ditch it, or otherwise make sure it finds its way into the "round file," otherwise known as the garbage can. If, for some reason, they are compelled to respond, they often do so in the most callous way imaginable. The lengths to which companies have gone to immunize themselves to our heartfelt letters is covered wonderfully in a book by John Bear, PhD, titled *Send This Jerk the Bedbug Letter* (Ten Speed Press, 1996). In his book, Dr. Bear relates the story of a tired business executive who was plagued by bedbugs on a luxury train trip. After writing to the company, the man received a deeply apologetic reply assuring him that it had never happened before and that all measures were being taken to make sure it never happened again.

Included with the letter was the man's original note, with a scrawl across the top: "Send this jerk the bedbug letter."

So if you want, you can write a letter. But the bottom line is that it's a lot of time and effort for little chance of a positive result.

CONVENTIONAL SOLUTION NUMBER TWO: GET YOUR ATTORNEY TO WRITE THE LETTER

When the personal letter fails to get a positive response, many books suggest an additional correspondence from your attorney to nudge the offending company into seeing things your way. Of course, this approach assumes that most of us have an attorney on our speed-dial who is just waiting for our call, eager to bill the big hourly fee for resolving a $200 dispute with a cell phone company.

The biggest downside of this approach is that once you get an attorney involved, your ability to negotiate with the company disappears. All correspondence thereafter is from their legal team to your legal team. (Yes, now you have a team of attorneys, and the bills to match.)

A lawyer friend of mine recently told me that in order to minimize costs, he handles letter requests from clients with boilerplate legal letters.

"Wait a minute," I said. "You mean that you respond to their form letter with your form letter?"

He nodded.

What you've really got, then, when you ask your attorney to write a letter, are two computers spitting canned threats and platitudes at each other until…what? Hell freezes over? However long it would take for the digital dialogue to conclude is likely longer than any of us would want to wait to solve a simple customer service problem.

So it seems that what we're left with—in this day of outsourced customer service—is a situation where no amount of letter writing, from you or your attorney, is likely to have any effect. Of course, you might get lucky. But are you really willing to run your life based on luck?

CONVENTIONAL SOLUTION NUMBER THREE:
TAKE THEM TO COURT

The underlying threat of an attorney letter is that, because you've involved an attorney, you're willing to go to court. A lot of people get really excited about finally "having their day in court." I need to tell you, this is really not a good idea, for several reasons.

Reason A: The bad news is that going to court is time-consuming and expensive. "That's the point," you say. "We want to cost them money." Yes, going to court is time-consuming and expensive for the company, but disproportionately so for you. They have better attorneys, lots of time, and boatloads of money. Unless you are John D. Rockefeller, you can't really afford the attorney you have, you are already overscheduled, and you don't have money to burn.

Companies are aware of this. They bet that, when decision day comes, you won't be willing to take off from work—and spend more money on attorneys—on the outside chance that you might win a small judgment.

Of course, if we're talking about tens of thousands of dollars, it could be worth it. However, most consumer disputes average less than $1,000. That means small claims court, and that you are likely going to have to take a lot of time off because the legal process is so slow. You can also bet that their lawyers can, and will, twist you into a tizzy before they agree to give you a nickel. They will delay and delay, so that you stew and stew, until you decide it isn't worth it and give up. This is because, more than anything, regardless of the amount at stake, they don't want to set a precedent of having people win judgments against them. It's unhealthy—for the corporation.

Reason B: The really bad news is that you might not be able to take them to court at all, unless you want to spend a lot of time in Delaware, Nevada, or the Cayman Islands. Buried in the owner's manual, purchase agreement, or EULA may be a legal clause declaring that all disputes will be handled in the jurisdiction of the state or nation in which the company was incorporated. This means that if you want to take them to court, you may be required to file your case in their home-town, whether it's Dover or New Delhi.

This is particularly true if you:

- ordered something by mail, catalog, or the Internet,
- are dealing with a national or an international company, or
- signed a contract, or agreed to a EULA, that reads, "…all disputes will be settled according to the laws of (their jurisdiction)."

Few of us are willing to spend a week overseas just to straighten out a warranty problem. (On the other hand, a week or two on the island of Grand Cayman could be quite enjoyable, even if you don't get your situation resolved in your favor.)

Reason C: Here's the worst news of all: you could lose. Sure, you're in the right. Absolutely, you were the one wronged. Of course, you have all the evidence. It doesn't matter. Civil court is a strange place where right and wrong are often irrelevant to the eventual decision of the court. Cases are decided on the rules of arcane and often illogical civil statutes that don't make sense to us common folk. Adding insult to injury, the loser in the case is often required to pay the legal and court fees of the winner. That means that if you went to court for an $800 claim, you could end up pay-ing many times that to cover the attorney fees of the company that screwed you in the first place!

CONVENTIONAL SOLUTION NUMBER FOUR:
WRITE IT OFF YOUR TAXES

I call this the "I don't believe I'm really right" solution.

As anyone who's ever filed their taxes knows, you don't get dollar for dollar when you write something off. "Writing it off" means you deduct the misdeed as a loss against your per-sonal income. Even if it is the type of loss that is allowed (not all losses are deductible), even if you itemize, and even if you have enough income to offset the loss, you still don't get more than 40¢ on the dollar in return. This is because every dollar you deduct in income decreases your tax by only 40¢, and only if you're in the highest tax bracket. If you're in a lower tax bracket, the news is worse. At 28 percent, you're saving just more than 25¢ in taxes for every dollar you got screwed out of. That's a hard pill for me to swallow. How about you?

CONVENTIONAL SOLUTION NUMBER FIVE: JUST FORGET ABOUT IT

Wait a minute: it's your money! And you're not a quitter. Otherwise, you wouldn't have turned the first page of this book, let alone read this far. Besides, I'm going to tell you over and over that you should only try to get what you're due, not change the world. Also, there's no escaping the knowledge that if they've done it to you, they'll do it to someone else and that you just might, by the time you've finished this book, have the ability not only to help yourself, but others, too.

Now—at the risk of sounding as though I'm contradicting myself—forgetting about it is often the best solution. In the next chapter, you'll find out why. You'll also take the first steps in learning about The Unscrewed Solution and how it can help you get what you deserve without waiting, going to court, writing it off, or giving up.

First, another Unscrewed True Story.

UNSCREWED TRUE STORY

The Hidden Interest Bump

I've been with the same bank now for more than a decade. For the most part, they've been very easy to deal with and have taken good care of my family. My wife and I have several accounts with them: our main checking account, a household expenses account, savings accounts for both kids, two credit cards, and a revolving credit line. It's that last account that started all the trouble a while back.

Credit lines are similar to credit cards, except that you write checks on them, and they usually don't cost you anything except for the interest on any money you borrow. Just like a credit card, once you're carrying a balance, there's a minimum monthly payment, but you can also pay off the entire amount if you want, to avoid paying interest.

I use this account for several purposes, frequently borrowing and repaying—sometimes in large amounts.

I was doing my end-of-year tax preparation for my accountant, when I noticed something unusual with the credit line account. According to the December statement, the interest rate had jumped from its normal 5.25 percent or so (prime plus 1.5 percent) to an astonishing 24 percent!

To be entirely honest, I don't check the interest rate on my accounts with each monthly statement, particularly on a credit line. I just make payments to avoid paying interest, and borrow money when I think it makes better financial sense than taking it out of some other investment. I couldn't understand what had happened. I searched through the year's statements for some notification that the interest rate had changed, but found nothing. What I did find was that it had been that way for at least six months and that I had paid almost *five times* the interest that I should have for that period.

I was sure it was a mistake that would be easily clarified with a call to the banker I'd been dealing with for so many years. My call was answered promptly. The receptionist told me that, as of the previous week, my banker was no longer with the bank. As an alternative, I was given the number of the bank's Credit Center. I jotted down the number, but had to run to a meeting, so the call would have to wait.

An hour or so later, during a break, I walked out to the parking lot of the building where the meeting was being held to get some sun. Reaching into my pocket, I discovered the note with the Credit Department's number on it. I figured, *What the heck, I've got ten minutes. Why not put it to good use and get this thing straightened out.*

I dialed the number and got a voice mail greeting: "Press 1 for English, 2 for…" I was told that "calls are recorded for training purposes." I made my way through the voice mail maze and was in music cue for an "expected wait of three minutes."

Almost five minutes later, and halfway through our break, someone clicked on the line. "This is Simon. How may I help you?"

"Hi, Simon," I said, introducing myself. "By the way, do you have an agent number?" (Later, you'll learn that this is one of the most important questions you can ask when dealing with a customer service representative.)

"Sure." He gave me the number. As I was running out of time, I briefly explained the situation and asked that it be corrected.

"I'm sorry. I can't do that," was Simon's reply.

"Why?" I asked.

"You see," he replied, "there wasn't a mistake. It's our policy that when the minimum payment is not made on an account that the interest rate on that account is increased."

"I'm not sure what you're talking about, Simon. I've paid that account down to zero at least three times this year."

"I see that," he said. "This concerns the July payment. I show a large payment on June 15, and then another rather large payment on July 22. However, there was a minimum payment due on July 1 that wasn't paid."

"So you're telling me that I missed a payment?"

"Yes. There was a payment due on July 1. There's a ten-day grace period. If it's not paid by then, the account is in default and the interest rate penalty kicks in."

He made it sound as though it were a pressure safety valve on my water heater. "But when you add up the June and July payments, I paid ten times the minimum payment for July."

"That's right, but neither of those payments was within the July payment grace period."

"Can't you just apply part of the June payment as an advance payment of the July payment?"

"No, I'm sorry, but I can't. That's not our policy."

I could see people heading back into the meeting. "But that doesn't make sense."

"I'm sorry, sir. If you don't like our policies, you can always take your business elsewhere."

One thing a customer service employee should never do is tell the truth about his or her desire to unload problem customers.

Something had to be done.

"Let me get this straight. It is your company's policy to turn away a good customer, someone who has done hundreds of thousands of dollars of business with your bank for more than a decade, by quintupling his interest rate? And that customer's only recourse is to take his business elsewhere?"

"That's not what I said," Simon said.

"But that is what you said," I replied mildly. "You told me to take my business elsewhere. And if we go back to the tape, we'll hear you say those exact words, which I will be sure to quote in my letter to the bank's executive offices this afternoon."

"What do you mean?"

"I'm going to fax a letter to the Executive Office this afternoon, letting them know exactly what you told this good customer to do. I'm going to prominently feature your name in the first paragraph as the person who told me to take my business elsewhere. It will say that Simon—agent 3154—told me that I should close all my accounts with your bank and go across the street with my business."

There was silence on the other end of the line.

"I think we're done here for now, Simon. I've got to go. Why don't you take some time to rethink this and call me back?"

I gave him my cell phone number and hung up. I switched off the ringer and returned to my meeting. About twenty minutes later, my phone vibrated.

A couple of hours later, when the meeting adjourned, I was finally able to retrieve my voice mail messages. There were two. The first was from Simon, apologizing profusely for mistreating me. "I certainly don't want you to get the impression that we don't value your business," he said.

The second voice mail was from the vice president in charge of consumer banking. He assured me that his company had made an error, that my account should not be subject to the automatic interest adjustment policy, and that they were refunding all of the interest charged, including the interest on the interest, although that might take them a few days to calculate.

Sure enough, I checked my account online just two days later, and there was a large credit, which actually gave me a positive balance on the account. I wondered silently whether they would pay me interest on that. *Probably not*. But with little effort and just the right words, I'd gotten what I deserved. The next few chapters will teach you the finer points of how you, too, can get what you deserve.

THE UNSCREWED SOLUTION

THE FIVE Ps

You've been screwed! You're angry, you're pissed off, and you want revenge. You ask, "What can I do?"

First of all, I want to say that I'm sorry that you've become trapped in the vortex of disappearing customer service. However, there is good news. Help is on the way. The solution to your problem is right in your hands. Relax for an hour or two, read the next few chapters, and you'll find out what to do to get what you deserve, and exactly how to get it.

The great fictional detective Sherlock Holmes once said, "When you have eliminated the impossible, whatever remains, however improbable, must be the truth." The same principle applies to getting yourself Unscrewed. Once we've eliminated all conventional solutions as viable routes to winning satisfaction, all we're left with is an unconventional solution: The Unscrewed Solution.

What makes this approach unconventional is that its success does not depend upon your ability to shout, stomp your feet, threaten holy terror, or spit from great distances. You are not required to commit crimes, dance on rooftops, or otherwise risk life or limb. You need not have great acting ability, a sprinter's speed, or skill in forging documents. Neither are you required to write pleading letters—waiting patiently for a response—or pay for professional assistance.

Unlike tired conventional solutions, this solution requires neither great patience nor perseverance. (Time equals money, and you've already lost enough of that.) In most cases, you will be able to Unscrew a situation in a matter of hours, if not minutes.

Even though I'm the one who developed this system, I'm still surprised at how quickly these techniques can turn around a situation. While I was in the middle of writing this book, I received a call from a friend. She had spent several months haggling with a cell phone company over an incorrect bill, then finally decided to call me for help. After talking with her for a few minutes and asking a few questions, I turned my attention to the errant company and implemented one of my techniques. In less than ten minutes, the vice president of customer relations called my friend, corrected the bill, and apologized for the error. She said to me, "That's amazing! Is it magic?"

Of course, there was nothing magical about it. As I'll demonstrate in the following chapters, getting what you deserve is more Archimedes than Houdini: you just need to know what lever to apply and where.

OK, I'll admit up front that some of the techniques are more than a little unconventional and are likely to knock a company representative or two off balance. That's the point! From now on, we don't blindly line up into the customer service cattle chute they've prepared for us. We do the unexpected.

I was recently asked whether my unconventional methods have ever elicited the crudely conventional threat of bodily harm, and was pleased to answer that in more than ten years of using these techniques, I've not once been physically threatened. As evidence, I point to a complete set of natural teeth and an absence of major scars. The peaceful, though often reluctant, reaction to these techniques can be credited to the underlying principle that we are engaged in a business dispute, not a personal confrontation. Personal comments and physical threats are not part of The Unscrewed Solution.

HIDE BEHIND TREES

More than two hundred years ago, our country's revolutionaries understood that to prevail against the better-trained and better-equipped armies of King George, they needed to change the rules of warfare. Instead of fighting by appointment on a specified field of battle, they hid behind trees and ambushed the Redcoats at every opportunity. Those ragtag patriots refused to play by the rules set down by their opponents.

We can learn a lot from those colonial revolutionaries. To successfully combat an unresponsive company, we need to find our own ways to hide behind trees and ambush the opposition. We must not play according to *their* rules: we must choose our own time and place to take them on.

Many of the true stories told in this book are my own. Others I heard firsthand from people who had been taken advantage of and only wanted to get what they deserved. As a reporter on the front lines of the consumer complaint battleground, I had observed the deliberate decline of corporate responsiveness and the rise of the adversarial atmosphere we know today. I also learned what worked—and what didn't.

I read numerous consumer books and "fight-back" news articles. None of them mentioned one simple principle I have discovered that was extraordinarily effective in getting a fair resolution to a consumer problem: companies will act only in a manner that will benefit the bottom line. In other words, to get what you deserve, you must convince your opponent that helping you will be to his or her advantage. (Doing this, of course, is easier written than done.)

However, once I understood that basic concept, I was able to develop a number of straightforward, though often unorthodox, techniques that are amazingly effective in getting my point across. Once you fully understand them, you will be equipped to take on even the most misguided management.

Not all of the techniques are appropriate for all occasions. Part of the process involves evaluating your situation to determine the best course of action. Knowing what *not* to do is often just as important as knowing what to do.

Like the colonists fighting their British oppressors, those who employ The Unscrewed Solution change the rules of engagement. Companies expect customers to behave like good schoolchildren. They've given you instructions and expect you to obey. Luckily for them, most of us do. Unluckily for them, once you understand The Unscrewed Solution, the only time you're going to play according to their rules is with that first call to Customer Service, when you give them a chance to do the right thing. But if they make it clear that's not going to happen, you will play a different game, with rules that fit your needs and your goals, not theirs.

THE FIVE Ps
The Unscrewed Solution is not complex. There are five fundamental elements, The Five Ps: The Unscrewed Principle, The Unscrewed Purpose, The Unscrewed Promise, The Unscrewed Power Tools, and The Unscrewed Plan.

The First P: The Principle
The Unscrewed Solution has one underlying principle upon which all the strategies and techniques rely:

A company will do only what is in its financial self-interest.

In other words, "It's all about the money." To get what you deserve, you must provide a resolution to your situation that both satisfies your needs and is apparently beneficial to the company's bottom line. I know that sounds as though it's a contradiction, but it isn't.

The Second P: The Purpose
The Unscrewed Solution is about getting back the only thing that companies and their employees really care about: the money. Unless we're talking about a company that's dump-

ing toxic chemicals into the playground, we can have only one purpose:

The purpose is to reclaim money, assets, or equity while minimizing time and effort.

I know it sounds unemotional. That's the point. Emotion has no place in a business negotiation, at least on our side of the table.

The Third P: The Promise

Although The Unscrewed Promise does not depend upon your ability to shout or scream, it does depend upon your ability to make one point absolutely clear:

"It will cost much more to ignore me than to take care of me, and I am willing to spend an unlimited amount of time and energy to get what I'm due."

This is the statement that turns the tables on the conventional customer-business relationship.

The Fourth P: The Power Tools

As we've discussed, the corporate community hides behind bastions of voice mail, contract companies, and small print. That's why you need The Unscrewed Power Tools. Here's what they are:

The Unscrewed Power Tools are five technologies and one nontechnical method that you use to leverage your position with your opponent.

The Power Tools are not exotic high-tech devices, inventory from Home Depot, or part of a torturer's kit bag. They are ordinary communication tools. What makes them powerful is how we use them.

The Fifth P: The Plan

The Unscrewed Plan is your road map to success, which you have created based on your research and chosen implementation of The Unscrewed Solution:

The Unscrewed Plan is designed to recover what you are due; it includes an acceptable goal, adversary research, a specific strategy, a realistic timeline, and an honest assessment of the situation.

You will use your plan (also known as your road map or your cheat sheet) during the implementation phase.

In upcoming chapters, we take a closer look at each of the Five Ps and how they work together to get you what you deserve. Before that, I'd like to share another story.

UNSCREWED TRUE STORY

The Shady Auto Shipper

A little more than ten years ago, I flew to California one weekend and finally convinced my girlfriend, Hali, to move to Hawaii and marry me. Over the next month and a half, she boxed up her belongings and shipped them via slow boat to Honolulu.

The only possession she couldn't fit in a cardboard banker's box was her 1985 Volkswagen Golf, named Otto. It would have to be sent with a freight forwarding company. Hali went through the Yellow Pages and found an outfit that claimed to ship cars to Hawaii for less than half the price of the mainstream moving companies. She didn't want to burden her fiancé with more moving costs than necessary, so she called up the A-1 Auto Moving Company.

Sure enough, they were willing to ship her car for her, the very next week, for the advertised price, about $1,000. All she'd need to do was give them a $500 cash deposit and they'd reserve a space on the next ship out. The timing was perfect. She was going to leave on her own flight at about the same time. It would mean that her car would get to Hawaii only a few days after she herself arrived. She'd be looking for a job once she got there, so she didn't want to be without a car for too long.

Hali drove down to the docks and gave the manager, Mike, a $500 money order. She was instructed to bring her car down the following week so that it could be immediately loaded onto the ship. Seven days later, Hali handed her car keys to the dockside attendant, took a taxi to the airport, and flew away to begin her new life in paradise.

The first few days in her new home were spent unpacking all of the boxes she'd shipped previously and getting to know her new surroundings. After a week had passed with no call to announce the arrival of her beloved Otto, Hali called A-1 in California. After Hali spent a few minutes on hold, Mike was on the line. She asked about her car. He apologized and explained that there hadn't been room on the ship that day after all and that her car was still on the dock in Oakland.

Alarmed, but reassured to hear that her car was OK, Hali asked, "When will you be able to send it?"

Mike coughed into the phone and said, "Well, we're pretty backed up right now. It will probably be several weeks before another space opens up."

"I need my car," Hali pleaded. "Isn't there something you can do?"

"I'm sorry," Mike said, unapologetically. "All the other slots are reserved for dealers, and it's our policy never to bump a commercial contract."

"But you promised me that you'd have my car to me this week!" said Hali, now almost in tears.

"As I said, it's our policy. If you'll read our contract, you'll see that we don't make any guarantees about delivery dates."

It appeared that she was stuck. Hali hung up the phone. After fuming for a half hour, she thought to call a mainstream mover. Surprisingly, the big outfit said they would be happy to ship her car for her, and could do it almost immediately for not much more than A-1 was asking. Sympathizing with her predicament, they even offered to pick the car up from the A-1 lot for her. Hali was elated. She called Mike at the A-1 office and told him the good news. He didn't seem to share her joy at solving the shipping dilemma. He said he'd release the car to the new company, but that he was unable to return her deposit, as he'd already booked a space on a ship three weeks later.

"Can't you cancel it?" Hali asked incredulously.

"No can do."

There has to be a way, thought Hali. "I'll talk to them."

"No can do," he repeated.

She didn't believe him. "Why?" She asked. "What's the name of the ship? What's the name of the shipping company?"

"I'm not going to give you privileged information. Besides, it doesn't matter," Mike shot back. "You signed a contract! I'm not going to give you back your deposit. *You're* the one who's changing *your* mind. Just make sure the other guys pick your car up by 5:00 today or I'll charge you storage fees." *Click*.

Hali was stunned. Not only did she not have her car, but the moving company was also going to cheat her out of $500. When I arrived home a few hours later, she told me the story.

Something had to be done.

I grabbed a POG (passion fruit–orange–guava juice, really divine), and went out to the lanai (porch) to ponder the problem. I reviewed the contract and the advertising brochures that Hali had received when she dropped off her car at the A-1 lot. They didn't appear to be a big outfit: there was only one office. They specialized in shipping cars from the West Coast to Hawaii and Asia. It seemed as though they did a lot of business, enough that they had a national toll-free number to take orders.

That gave me an idea. Most consumers don't realize that a toll-free number is free only for the *customer*. The business is paying a long-distance fee, and it's often a pretty steep rate, especially if the caller is overseas (and that includes Hawaii). The business is usually charged a connect fee of a dollar or so, and then per-minute charges on top of that. Of course, if the company is making a lot of sales, then the cost of the call barely dents the bottom line.

The next morning after breakfast, I called A-1 and asked for the owner of the company. Mike came on the line. I let him know who I was and politely asked him to refund Hali's deposit. He refused. At that point, I shared with him my version of The Unscrewed Promise.

"Mike," I said, "$500 isn't a lot of money to us. However, this just isn't right. So I'm letting you know now that I'm going to do whatever I can to make sure that you don't get to keep Hali's $500. In fact, your bad behavior may end up costing you many times the amount of the deposit."

Mike asked the inevitable question: "You going to take me to court?" He snickered. "It'll cost you more to fly over here for the court date than to just give this up. Oh sure, I'm real scared."

At that point, I understood that this was not the first time that Mike had refused to return a deposit and gotten away with it. Folks who had moved across an ocean weren't likely to return to California to file a suit in small claims court to get back $500. He thought he was on pretty safe ground. The itch on the back of my neck told me that Mike could have ripped off dozens of people throughout the years.

"Mike, all I ask is that you take down my home phone number in case you reconsider."

Silence. Then he snickered again. "Sure." I gave him the number. End of conversation.

I went down the hall to my home office and sat down in front of my computer. I called the new mover and made sure they'd already picked up Hali's car. They had, and they offered to help in any way they could to see that Otto got to the islands as quickly as possible. Evidently, they knew about Mike's shady reputation. I thanked them for their professionalism and courtesy. (I really do like working with legitimate businesses.)

I opened my fax software program and entered A-1's toll-free phone number. I then created a one-page blank fax and

instructed the fax software to fax it to the toll-free number—
again and again. I clicked the "send" button and listened as
my fax line found a dial tone. I heard a voice answer, the fax
screamed, and then the line hung up. Ten seconds later, the
PC dialed again. A voice answered, cursed, and hung up.

At $1 per connection, it would take some time to have any
great effect on Mike's bottom line. However, that didn't take
into account the sales he was losing because other customers
couldn't get through. I actually felt good about that, though.
Perhaps I was saving someone else some grief.

The only question in my mind was whether Mike was
bright enough to connect the toll-free assault with his despi-
cable treatment of the newest island girl. I put the odds at
sixty-forty…against Mike.

He was smarter than I gave him credit for. Just two hours
later, my home phone rang. It was Mike. He was *very* angry

"Hey, [blank]," he said. "What the [blank] do you think
you're doing? You're costing me a lot of money."

"You cost *us* a lot of money," I replied. "I guess you'll
have to sue me."

"What do you want?"

"All I want is my fiancée's deposit back."

"OK, I'll mail it to you."

"No. I'll have someone pick it up at your place in half an
hour. If it's not ready, we'll talk again tomorrow, but the
phone will keep ringing. Deal?"

"You haven't heard the end of this!" he blustered.

"Do we have an agreement?" I asked.

"Yes," he said and hung up.

I called our new mover, explained the situation, and
asked if they would mind picking up the check for me. They
obliged. Eight days later, Otto arrived in our driveway, with a
$500 check in the glove compartment.

And yes, it cleared.

THE UNSCREWED PRINCIPLE

Acompany will do only what is in its financial self-interest.
Half a century ago, we were told that a few emerging
"multinational" corporations would become lawless
international entities, without conscience or community.
Today, we are no longer talking about a handful of multinational oil or car companies. Our home-grown capitalist
economy has leapfrogged into a global capitalist economy
where *every* company is, in some way, multinational. Instead
of a few elite megacorporations crossing borders, we now
have tens of thousands of companies with international interests, dependence, and influence. There is hardly a listing in
the Yellow Pages that doesn't sell internationally or depend
on imported resources.

WHAT'S THE PROBLEM?
Does global capitalism make the entire world a free market
for goods and services? Yes. With the Internet, even the small-
est manufacturer can market globally.

Does this global opportunity provide an international
pool of material and labor resources? Yes. Companies can
search the globe for the lowest cost materials and the cheap-
est labor.

Does a global market enhance competition? In general,
yes. Competitors are no longer just across the street: they're
across the ocean as well.

All the preceding statements are true. They are also the reasons that consumers feel cut off from and ignored by many of those same companies.

Ironically, this is the inevitable endgame of U.S. capitalism. This is what we have strived for. It is what we have found at the end of the rainbow. Minimizing costs means finding the lowest-cost laborers, wherever they may be. That translates into customer service phone centers in third-world countries with contract representatives who don't work for the company you're calling about and who have no interest in that company's products, other than performing well on the customer service contract.

Economic globalization, combined with the franchise economy, has erased any sense of corporate citizenship in our communities. Sure, their logos are on the backs of our Little League players. We read about sponsorships of the local symphony or contributions to area charities. That's just good marketing. What we rarely see is a company willing to sacrifice profit for no purpose other than the good of their employees, customers, or the communities they inhabit. There's good reason for that. If they did, their stockholders would rebel. Investors rightfully expect a positive return on their investments. They often look at cash giveaways, unearned discounts, or other benefits as irresponsible management, rather than good customer service.

Accordingly, every management decision is measured against how it will affect the company's bottom line. Contributions to charity are part of the marketing budget. Contributions to unhappy customers? There's no line item for that.

Lose you as a customer, they can find ten more. Ask ten of your friends to stop shopping at that store because of the way you were treated, and twenty more are drawn in the front doors by the television and newspaper ads, placed by the national agency.

In the current state of economic Darwinism—where the customer has become a commodity, rather than a capital asset—there is only one way an individual can have any leverage. In order to be heard, and to have a chance of getting your way, you must convince the company you are dealing with that you have the ability to positively or negatively affect the only thing they care about: their bottom line.

In the new global economy, only the most efficient, most profitable companies will survive in this worldwide battleground of economic adversaries.

In previous chapters, we discussed the many reasons that corporations often aren't concerned about you as a complaining customer. Add to that the pressures of the new global economy, and companies are left with few alternatives.

In deciding to swap "The customer is always right" for a business model based on "There's another one where that one came from," they've tossed the numbers into a simple profit-and-loss equation and decided that it will cost them less to replace you than to deal with you. More than economic recession, globalism, or franchising, this malevolent turn of mathematics is the primary reason why we are in a customer service crisis and why we consistently find ourselves getting screwed by the companies with whom we do business.

CHANGING POINT OF VIEW

The secret to The Unscrewed Solution is to turn that equation on its ear. It's time to stop thinking of yourself as a "wronged" customer and begin thinking like a business. *Instead of asking your adversary to make a difficult customer service decision, put your adversary in the position to make an easy business decision.*

When you start thinking in those terms and apply The Unscrewed Principle, the answer to the customer service dilemma becomes clear. Because a company's decision not to deal with you is based solely on the relative cost, the obvious solution is to change the cost-benefit equation. If the company is going to do only what is in its financial best interest, then you must convince that company that it is more profitable to satisfy you than to leave you unsatisfied. It can also be stated in the reverse: you must make it more costly for the company to ignore you than to take care of you.

Whichever way you look at it, the result is the same. The net cost to the company is higher if you are not satisfied. That cost can be direct, such as a loss of business, which can take many forms. Sometimes the potential loss is personal to the company representative with whom you are dealing. Other times, the bottom line of the company is directly threatened. Whatever the case, when it becomes clear to a company that it will suffer less by taking care of you than ignoring you, it will make the financially correct decision, and you will get what you deserve.

I cannot overstate the importance of this basic principle in achieving your ultimate goal. It is the foundation of everything else in this book. Your ability to implement The Unscrewed Solution depends entirely on how well you apply The Unscrewed Principle in each unique situation.

Every company is different, and every situation is different. I know it may seem incredible that we, as individuals, can be powerful enough to affect the bottom line of a megacorporation. But we can. I've done it hundreds of times.

In the next chapter, we'll look at the second P, the purpose. First, though, is a story that demonstrates how simply The Unscrewed Principle can be applied.

UNSCREWED TRUE STORY
The Bait-and-Switch Tire Store

My wife, Hali, is a trusting soul. It's a quality that I personally find quite endearing, but it can get her into a lot of trouble.

A while ago, I noticed that the tires on Hali's SUV were down to the wear bars. We were heading into winter, so I thought it was important to get new tires. I was preparing for a seminar and really didn't want to spend all afternoon at the tire store.

Hali said, "No problem! I'll do it."

I sent her off to Blue State Tires to get a set of four new Michelin tires—exactly what was on the car at the time; that set had served us well.

After a couple of hours, Hali returned, beaming. "Come take a look, honey," she said. "I got us a real deal."

Frankly, I'd never heard of Michelin tires going on sale anywhere. I was curious; also, the alarm on my "screw" detector had begun to clang. I followed Hali to the driveway, where she proudly pointed out her brand new set of four tires.

"The guy at the store said they were just as good as Michelins. And they cost $30 less per tire. Isn't that great? Aren't you proud of me for being such a smart shopper?"

It was a delicate situation, similar to the one a man faces when a woman asks, "Does this dress make me look fat?" I looked at her. She was so happy and so proud of herself. I was peeved with the sleazy salesperson who'd sold her crap—and put me in the situation of having to tell my wife and best friend that she'd been ripped off. While not the classic "bait-and-switch" routine, the salesman had clearly led her to believe that the knockoff tires were just as good as the Michelins I had sent her to buy.

And I felt angry at myself for sending her into that situation entirely unprepared for what she might face. I opted for the straight-line approach.

"Honey," I said, "I know what he told you, but it isn't true." Hali looked crestfallen. "You believed him. It's not your fault. I'll take care of it." I gave her a hug.

I went to my computer, and after five minutes had the scoop on the four rubber imposters mounted on Hali's Lexus.

Although it's true that many companies will do the right thing when given a chance to correct a wrong, Blue State Tires wasn't one of them.

I called the number on my wife's receipt and asked for the manager. "That's me," said the artificially deep voice on the other end of the phone. The guy sounded as though he were rehearsing for a radio job. "What can I do for you?"

"What's your name?" I asked.

"Mitch. Who are you?"

"My name is Ron Burley. You just installed four new tires on my wife's car."

"Uh, yes. She got a great deal."

"I don't think so," I replied.

"Now, Ron, those are excellent tires."

"I don't think so, and neither does *Consumer Reports, Car & Driver*, or the National Highway Safety Administration."

"I don't know about that, but—"

I cut him off. "Mitch, my wife asked for Michelins. I believe she even handed you a piece of paper with the model number. You took advantage of her naïveté and talked her into a set of knockoff tires that won't last 20,000 miles. So I'm going to send her back down there, and I expect you to put on the Michelins."

"I can't do that," Mitch said. "Our sales receipt clearly states that if the customer drives the vehicle off the property, the tires are nonrefundable. After all, I couldn't very well sell them as new, could I?"

Mitch had apparently convinced himself that this was a compelling argument. No doubt, it had many times turned back a questioning customer.

Something had to be done.

"That's not my problem, Mitch," I said calmly. "I'd like to come down there to talk with you about this, if you don't mind."

"Well, sure. But as I said, there's nothing we can do. I assure you, though, they're fine tires."

"I'll see you in half an hour, Mitch."

"Okay. I'll be here."

While on the phone with Manager Mitch, I'd pretty well assessed the situation and come up with a strategy.

I grabbed the Yellow Pages and found the full-page display ad for Mitch's competitor, located just across the street from his store. I scanned it into my computer and printed a dozen copies. I grabbed a stapler and a file folder, and I headed out the door to my car. I called to Hali to meet me back at the tire store in about twenty minutes.

On the way to Blue State Tires, I made one stop—at my ATM—where I picked up $240 in $20 bills. I stapled each of the bills to one of the copies of the competitor's ad. I put the whole pile in the manila file folder. Five minutes later, I pulled into the parking lot for Blue State Tires. Hali was already there.

It was a busy day at Blue State. More than a dozen folks were lined up, waiting for service. I walked to the end of the counter and asked a man thumbing through a pile of invoices if the manager was available. "That's me," he said.

"Hi, Mitch," I said, sticking my hand over the counter to shake his. "I'm Ron Burley. We just spoke on the phone."

He shook my hand and looked at me curiously. "At the risk of sounding like a broken record, I'll tell you again that I'm sorry, but we can't refund an order that's left the premises. It's our policy."

It's our policy? He'd just tossed gasoline on my nice little campfire.

"Mitch, I'm not here to debate with you." I placed the file folder on the counter in front of him so that the contents would be facing his direction. "I'm here to make one last request for you to simply put on the tires that my wife asked for. If you can't do that"—I opened the file folder and glanced at the waiting line—"I'll walk out of here, telling as many of those people in line exactly how we've been treated this afternoon. I'll hand them a copy of your competitor's ad and ask them if, for $20, they wouldn't mind going across the street to get their tires."

Mitch's mouth dropped open. He looked like a man who had just missed the lottery by one digit. His eyes scanned the top sheet, fixating on the stapled $20 bill.

"I've got a dozen of these," I said. "Walking out of here, I may not get the tires I want, and it might cost me a couple of hundred dollars to see those folks walk across the street. But you know what? I'll feel a lot better knowing that I saved a few people from having to go through what we've been through today."

Mitch was looking at the line of people at the counter and tapping the tip of a pen on the countertop.

"So what'll it be, Mitch? You put the correct tires on the car, or we see exactly how much business I can hand to the other guys as I walk out the door."

Mitch looked me straight in the eye and smiled thinly. "Ron, I'm sorry for the misunderstanding. Please have your wife pull her car around back. We'll be happy to take care of her right away."

Back home, I unstapled the $20 bills. My wife arrived an hour after I did, rolling into the driveway on a set of four new Michelin tires.

THE UNSCREWED PURPOSE

The Unscrewed Purpose is to reclaim money, assets, or equity while minimizing time and effort.

So you've been screwed by some corporation. They've taken your money, wasted your time, and possibly even wrinkled your reputation. You're angry. You're embarrassed and humiliated. You want to get even. You want to take some names and kick some ass!

It's the first reaction most of us have when we find out that we've been taken advantage of. We want more than our money back. We want someone to pay. We want the person responsible to feel personally the pain and humiliation that we have felt.

Give it up!

The first thing to learn about getting Unscrewed is that it is not about:

- screwing them back,
- getting a pound of flesh, or
- claiming an eye for an eye.

All of these goals fall under the general category of revenge. Although getting revenge may make you feel better, it doesn't actually further your goal of getting what you deserve. It's important to note that although we know revenge is not our goal, it is sometimes in our best interest for our adversary to believe it is. People driven by revenge will often do things that are beyond what a calm person considers reasonable or prudent. If your adversary thinks you are "just a little bit crazy," that can work to your advantage—just as long as you don't believe it yourself. Revenge has no value. It puts no money in your pocket. Even worse, it creates an adversary, who now may feel a need to retaliate.

Likewise, getting Unscrewed has nothing to do with:

- making people feel bad,
- getting somebody fired, or
- bankrupting a company.

These three goals fall under the general category of inflicting pain on a personal level. The universal human tendency to take pleasure in getting even means that we all, at some time and to some degree, get pleasure from someone else's pain. Get too much into that and it's sociopathic behavior. Moreover, threatening someone's livelihood is likely to get them pretty mad at you, creating an enemy where you really need an ally. At the least, it can cause them to marginalize you as crazy or a kook, virtually guaranteeing that you will not get what you deserve. It will bring the conversation to an immediate end, with you possibly blacklisted as a problem customer. It gives everyone an excuse to ignore you, no matter how legitimate your claim is. "Says right here, she's crazy. Ignore her."

We have all dealt with employees that we know have no business working in the position they are in. Some of us have even worked with, or for, some of those people. Just as with getting even, getting someone fired is not going to do anything positive for your economic position. It's also another opportunity to create an enemy. If the employee deserves to be fired, the best way to make sure that happens is to get what you deserve. The company might then realize that the employee is costing more money than he or she is worth. It might be a nice side effect, but "making sure the jerk loses his job" cannot be your goal.

As far as bankrupting the company, the bad news is that there is no way that you are going to be able to do any meaningful, long-lasting harm to an offending corporation. The really bad news is that if you tried, you'd probably be thrown in jail. We all know it's against the law to do intentional harm to another person. It's also illegal to do anything with the express intent of damaging the reputation of a business or its ability to do commerce. Some of the techniques you'll learn in this book purposely walk close to that line. It is very important to know where that line is, and not cross it. We will cover that in greater depth in later chapters.

Finally, you are not trying to:

- prove you're right, or
- win an apology.

Prove you're right? Get an apology? Could happen, though it's not likely. In any case, I'm not sure what it means when a company—a business enterprise licensed by the state—makes an apology to an individual. (I do know that most of the apologies I've received from companies haven't been worth the value of the electrons used to send them. Apologies are often meant to appease instead of paying what is due.)

Is the management of the company accepting fault?

Does it mean the company will change its ways?

That's not very likely and is too much to hope for. I agree that in a lot of cases, companies should change their ways. I'd go even further, to say that they should be required to take out full-page ads apologizing to customers they've screwed. Corporate officers who endorse exploitative practices should be canned, and company policies should be amended to prevent any reoccurrence.

There used to be a concept called corporate citizenship: a company would consider how its actions affected the communities in which it operated. Very few companies appear to consider themselves to be corporate citizens these days, and the debate about what is proper corporate citizenship is beyond the scope of this book.

We all get emotional about money. For many of us, our self-worth is tied up with how much we earn. We all work hard for what we earn and rightfully get angry when someone steals our dough. However, this emotionalism works against our purpose.

Taking a step back from our emotions is difficult. For thousands of generations, the proper response to a threat was to beat your chest, scream, yell, and wave a stick in the air. But in the modern world, we need to distance ourselves from the desire to dive through the phone, grab someone by the neck, and shake him silly. I know it's hard not to scream at that kid just out of college in the Loan Department at your bank who tells you they have no record of your payment and are foreclosing on your home—even though you have a copy of the canceled check in your hand. It's a lesson I learned the hard way.

UNSCREWED TRUE STORY

Screamers Never Prosper

Several years ago, I was putting together a real estate deal. The mortgage financing was contingent upon obtaining property and liability insurance. I put it on the back burner, and then I forgot about it. Just a few days short of closing, the bank called and asked if I could fax them proof of insurance. I already had the feeling that the seller might back out of the deal if given half a chance; I didn't want to give him one. He certainly wouldn't extend the closing date. So I had to get some insurance on the property…and quickly.

Feeling embarrassed, and not wanting to let the broker know that I'd completely spaced out on the insurance coverage, I told him, "Sure. I'll send it to you as soon as I get back to the office."

A friend had earlier given me the name of an insurance agent, Richard Carter, who had a reputation for expediting paperwork. It was about eleven in the morning when I dug out his phone number and gave him a call.

"Carter Insurance, Nancy speaking."

The receptionist explained that Mr. Carter was out of the office, but that he would be back in an hour or so. I mentioned that I had been referred by a mutual friend and had to act quickly.

"If I can ask you a few questions, we can probably get this taken care of for you this afternoon," Nancy said.

It took only a minute to give her the information on the project.

"I'll make sure he returns your call as soon as he gets in," Nancy assured me.

I was pretty busy for the next few hours, so it wasn't until after four in the afternoon that I realized that I'd not heard back from Mr. Carter, and that the bank was still waiting on my promised fax. I pulled over to the side of the road and got out my cell. I was already upset with myself for the insurance oversight. I had redirected my anger by the time Nancy answered the phone at Carter Insurance.

"Do you mind me asking what kind of business you're running there?" I demanded.

"Excuse me. Who is this?" It was Nancy.

"This is the guy you promised would get a phone call from your boss as soon as he got back to the office."

"I'm sorry. Your name?"

"So you not only forgot to give him the message, you've even forgotten my name. Are you always this sloppy with important clients?"

I could hear a quiver in her voice.

"I'm sorry," she said. "But something came up. If you could tell me your name, I'm sure that I can find someone to help you."

"Look here…Nancy. I'm at the wall on a multimillion-dollar real estate deal, and your inability to pass on a simple phone message just may lose it for me."

I could hear her shuffling through some papers. "Is this Mr. Burley?"

"Yes, and if I'm not mistaken, you're the one who promised me that your boss would get back to me hours ago. I trusted you—and him—to behave professionally. Instead, you've dropped the ball and have potentially cost me a lot of money."

"I'm very sorry, Mr. Burley." She was sobbing. "I passed your message to Mr. Carter, but he had to leave on an emergency. I'm not sure what the status is on your application."

"So your boss leaves and fails to tell anybody what's going on. Is that right?"

"I'm not sure. If you could just—" She was pleading.

I cut her off. "No. I can't. You just get hold of Mr. Carter and tell him that he'd better make something happen here or I'm going to let every one of my business associates know that he's a screwup."

I heard one last sob as I pressed the "end" button. I knew that I'd let my anger get the best of me. But I really didn't want to lose the deal. I also realized that it was really my fault and that it was unfair to take it out on the insurance company. But at the time, it didn't seem to matter. I just needed to get the deal done.

I sat there in my car for a few minutes, wondering what my next move should be. My cell phone rang. It was the insurance agent.

"Mr. Burley?" he asked. "This is Richard Carter."

"Yes," I said, with a tinge of disdain.

"Mr. Burley. I'm at Mercy Hospital. My daughter was in a car accident this afternoon."

"I'm sorry."

"What you don't know is that before I left, I faxed an insurance rider to your mortgage company."

"No. I didn't know that."

"Clearly, you didn't. Otherwise, you wouldn't have badgered my secretary to the point of tears."

"I'm sorry, Richard. It's just that this deal—"

He cut me off.

"Mr. Burley, I don't know what kind of businessperson you are. But your treatment of my employee tells me that you are certainly not the kind of person that I want to do business with. Therefore, I've called Emerald Realty and withdrawn our policy approval. You'll have to take your business elsewhere."

"Mr. Carter, I'm very sorry for coming on so strong with Nancy. I just got carried away with—"

He cut me off again.

"Frankly, I'm not interested in why you acted like such an ass. It's my right to do business with whomever I choose, and I choose *not* to do business with you. Good-bye."

The phone went silent. It didn't take more than a few seconds of honest self-reflection to realize that he was right. I had acted like an ass.

Nothing could be done.

There was no way I would be able to Unscrew myself from the problem I'd created. I called the realtor, who was quite confused about the whole situation. I explained that Carter would not be underwriting the policy.

"We still need to have that coverage in place by the close of business tomorrow," he said.

"I'll have it," I promised.

In fact, I was able to find another carrier the next morning, in time to close the deal. It cost me several hundred dollars more than the proposal from Carter Insurance. In the end, I considered it cheap tuition for several valuable lessons:

- You must be in the right. The foul-up was mine, and I would have been far better off admitting it and asking for help, instead of blaming someone else.

- Never make it personal: keep it about business. You cannot expect a businessperson to make a business decision when you make it personal.
- Control your anger. Little is accomplished by yelling or making threats. And, above all, never make the secretary cry. No one will ever do any favors for a bully.

That was the end of my career as a "screamer." It also highlights an important concept for all negotiations—that we don't want to do anything that will distract us from our goal or reduce our chances of getting it. A corporate apology is worthless and we can't really harm them, so the only legitimate goal is to reclaim our tangible property: money, assets, or equity. Or, to quote my younger brother, John, a millionaire, "He who gets the money, wins."

In many ways, the law treats corporations as individuals, as people. It's time that we, the real people, begin thinking like corporations. To fight them successfully, we need to be as cool and businesslike as they are. We need to be as focused on our objective. We need to be as dispassionate about the means. Most of all, we need to think the way a corporation thinks: all that matters is the money.

That said, there are some situations in which your goal might include more than just monetary compensation. As you'll read in a later Unscrewed True Story, "The UnPayroll Company," sometimes you'll need the offending company to write letters or make calls on your behalf, to clean up a mess they've made. These are valid requests, though getting a company to agree to them can often be much tougher than winning a strictly monetary goal.

Exactly how much money you are due is not always the amount on the receipt. It's fair to include shipping costs, money spent on a rental to replace a defective product, and, in some cases, even the cost of the loss of business. If you were bumped from a flight and had to buy meals and lodging, reimbursement of those costs would certainly be justifiable (though often not legally required).

THINK LIKE A BUSINESS

A Native American hunter was once asked his secret to success in tracking buffalo across the Great Plains. "I think like the buffalo," he said. "When I think like him, I know where he will be, and what he will do." Before the arrival of Europeans, Native Americans didn't hunt on horseback: they didn't have any horses. They hunted with stealth, often able to approach within feet of their prey, because dressed in sheepskin they weren't seen as a threat.

Most companies are like buffalo, grazing the economic landscape for ways to increase profit or otherwise improve the bottom line. If a company decides that you are irrelevant to their profitability, you will be ignored. A company will not pay attention to you until you become a threat to the bottom line.

When we are planning our strategy against a company, we need to think like that company, so that we understand what matters to it and how it will react when threatened. We need to get close to it, understand it, and, then and only then, implement our plan to recover what we are due.

Before you contact a company about a claim, know what you're going to ask for. The higher you set the bar, the less likely your chances are of getting over the hurdle. In some situations, it is an acceptable tactic to set a lofty goal and then negotiate down. Just make sure you don't set the bar so high that you convince your opponent that you are unreasonable.

The final consideration is whether a situation is worth the time and effort you are going to apply to it. Obviously, it would be illogical to spend an entire day trying to get back 50¢ you lost in a vending machine. Not all screwed-up situations, however, are that clear. In chapter 9, you will learn how to assess whether a situation is worth your time.

Here's another story in which the actual dollar value lost was minimal. However, the collateral loss—a small company's employer-employees relationship—was immense.

UNSCREWED TRUE STORY
The UnPayroll Company

In the 1990s, I got into…and then out of…the software business. I started a small software company, Broadcast Software International (BSI), by myself out of a spare bedroom. In just a few years, it had grown to be an enterprise with almost twenty employees.

The biggest headaches involved in running a small company are payroll and payroll taxes. Thankfully, there are a number of companies out there who will take care of the process for you, making payroll almost effortless. That is, if everything goes as planned.

Our payroll usually arrived by express mail on the first and fifteenth of each month. This story begins when we'd been with our payroll service, American Payroll, Inc., for more than a year. We had generally been satisfied. Most of our employees received just a receipt in the envelope, because they used the electronic deposit option: American Payroll automatically deposited the proper amount directly into their bank accounts.

The first of the month arrived. Halfway through the day, well after the usual morning express delivery, my business manager informed me that the payroll envelope had not arrived. Initial calls to the payroll company were met with an array of excuses.

Something had to be done.

What followed was a folly of immense proportions. It would have been comical, except that it broke the sacred trust between employer and employee.

The following is the text of the letter I faxed to the president of the payroll company.

Mr. James G. Hardcover
President & Chief Operating Officer
American Payroll
3 Washington Boulevard
Primrose, N.Y. 10010

Dear Mr. Hardcover:

I am about to share with you an amazing story: amazing because it's true and because it happened with your company.

Our company is a client of your BasicPay service, Western Regional Office. Four days ago, we noticed that our payroll had not been delivered on time, so I called the American Payroll BasicPay office. I spoke with Janet. Here's how the conversation went:

Ron: Hello, this is Ron Burley of BSI. We didn't get our payroll today.

Janet: Oh. Our records show that we dropped it off with Matt. Wait a minute. Do you have a mat? Like a doormat? That we could have put it under? Oh, hold on. [Puts me on hold and then returns one minute later.] My driver says we dropped it off with the regular woman on Thursday: short with dark, curly hair.

Ron: Well, our receptionist is blonde, and the only other person up front is our office manager. She's black and has dreadlocks.

Janet: Oh. Can we get you new checks in the morning?

Ron: Sure.

The next morning, the replacement payroll arrived, but the checks weren't signed. Then I was informed that the payroll that was lost had been drawn off of our company checking account, rather than the usual American Payroll payroll account. That meant that there were sixteen checks floating around somewhere that could be cashed off of our corporate account, and we hadn't even been notified. Janet said she would have told me, but forgot. So we immediately put a stop payment on the check numbers she gave me. Janet sent a fax confirmation of the stop-payment numbers.

I also spoke with Janet's supervisor, Carol, who treated the whole situation as if it were not important. She accused me of "blowing this out of proportion." I let her know that I take my relationship with my employees very seriously, and that for them to get their payroll a day late was a very serious matter.

Yesterday evening, one of my employees called me at home to tell me that his paycheck had been returned by the bank, marked "payment stopped." The problem, we finally figured out, was that the check numbers that Carol had given me were for the second set of checks. Therefore, I had dutifully put a stop payment on the replacement checks that we handed out to our staff.

Mr. Hardcover, I'm sure you understand that the contract between employer and employee is, most simply, a day's work for a day's pay. Because of the incompetence and arrogance of American Payroll's employees, I now have a staff who have lost faith in their employer's ability to fulfill that contract. I was forced to hold an emergency staff meeting this morning, where I issued additional replacement checks out of my personal checking account. I was also compelled to apologize to them for the embarrassment of having to explain to their creditors and bankers that they do not work for a scofflaw company.

The fallout from this could last months. Checks have bounced, credit ratings have been adversely affected, fees have been imposed, and relationships have come into question. All this because a couple of people in your regional office became so jaded that they forgot the importance of the service that they provide. They have evidently become so cavalier about their duties that they no longer care that people depend on them to do their work well.

When I got Carol on the phone this morning, I let her know how I feel and requested a call from her boss. Someone named Rebecca called. I let her know how I felt; she hung up on me. I was not using profanity or threatening her. I was just letting her know the importance of what was going on. Evidently, she didn't understand why someone might be upset after such a series of events, and didn't want to hear anything about it. I don't know whether this is acceptable policy at American Payroll, but if someone on my staff hung up on a client in that manner, she would be let go immediately.

Mr. Hardcover, I could just fire American Payroll and go somewhere else. Instead, I would like to help you make your company better. Someone, somewhere in your organization needs to remember that the work you do is very important. It is perhaps the most important aspect of any business.

My current request to BasicPay is as follows:
- A letter of indemnification to our bank regarding the missing checks;
- A letter to each member of my staff, apologizing for the cancellation of the wrong checks and an explanation for any creditors or financial institutions;
- Compensation for any fees or charges incurred by BSI or its employees; and
- The next twelve months of payroll service free for BSI(we will use the funds to throw a party for our employees, to begin rebuilding a damaged employer–employee relationship).

Given the series of events, I think that these requests are entirely within reason.

I cannot keep any of our employees from going to the media or to individual counsel regarding this series of events. However, if we can expeditiously move to address these issues, we may preempt such actions. If we can't, I'm sure we could sell this story to any one of the national tabloid publications for more than enough to cover the bank fees and the party.

I look forward to hearing from you.

Sincerely,

Ron Burley
President
Broadcast Software International

I know it seems incredible. If I hadn't experienced that episode firsthand, I would never have believed it happened.

Mr. Hardcover called within the hour.

"Is this true?" he asked.

"Every unfortunate event," I replied.

Sometimes, if you reach high enough in a company, you can find someone who understands the cost-benefit equation. I don't know whether Mr. Hardcover was as appalled as I was or really just concerned about the media exposure. Whatever his reasons, he was a good businessperson. He apologized for the fiasco and immediately agreed to all my requests. He even tossed in an additional $1,000 for the morale party.

THE UNSCREWED PROMISE

I t will cost much more to ignore me than to take care of me, and I am willing to spend an unlimited amount of time and energy to get what I'm due.

The Unscrewed Promise is your personal statement of The Unscrewed Principle and The Unscrewed Purpose. This is what you are going to say to the company to get your way. At first glance, that promise may appear to be more threat than promise. It is not, and cannot be. It is a simple pledge that you make to yourself, and your opponent, that you are willing to exercise your right of free speech to let the world know about how you have been treated, and that the net result of that will likely be a loss of revenue and reputation for the company.

The Promise takes the emotion out of the equation and places a simple business decision in front of the offending company. When presented with the choice—provide satisfaction to the squeakiest of wheels or face potential financial loss—most companies will make the most profitable decision: to satisfy you.

I do not state the Promise the same way every time. The Promise is a concept that is adapted to each individual situation and the technique that is used. The exact wording of the statement is not as important as the concept—that you are willing to exert an unlimited amount of time and effort to let others know how you have been treated and that the net result of that could be a loss of revenue for the offending company.

As has been mentioned earlier, and will be several times again, the Promise must not be stated as a direct threat to the company or an individual.

You cannot say in plain language, *"I intend to disrupt your sales and lose you business."* You could be sued for that. However, a subtle change turns the Promise into a powerful—and legal—personal statement: "I am going to exercise my free speech rights, and my duty as a member of this community, to let my fellow citizens know how I have been treated."

In this case, you are taking advantage of your constitutionally protected right of free speech. You are also fulfilling a solemn obligation to protect your neighbors and friends from scoundrels. It seems as though it's a small difference, I know, but it's an important difference. If you state that your specific intent is to take away business, that is not lawful. On the other hand, it is perfectly legal to let the company know your intention is to tell others to steer clear because "in your opinion" the company doesn't treat its customers well. You can even connect the dots for them by apologizing for the inevitable loss of business that may result from the performance of your civic duty.

In my own efforts, I have stated the Promise in several different ways. Here are my basic presentations.

CIVIC DUTY
"If we can't resolve this situation today, I will be compelled to warn as many people as possible about the way your company treats its customers. In the end, it may cost you ten or twenty times as much as just taking care of me today. I may not get a cent of it, but I'll certainly feel better, knowing that I have done my civic duty and may have saved many others the misfortune of doing business with your firm."

"Civic duty" makes the point that your actions will likely have a negative effect on the bottom line, though it's important to note that the wording is not *"I am going to make sure you lose customers."* In many states, that could be interpreted as a deliberate action to damage a business. The company might be able to sue you for loss-of-business damages. However, when you phrase it in terms of warning other people, the promise becomes a matter of your free speech and your obligation to protect your fellow citizens.

The altruistic final line is also important. Angry people often spit and yell, but eventually calm down. Idealists, activists, and other zealots are truth tellers for whom a situation such as this becomes a cause. And the last thing any business owner wants to become is someone's *negative* reason for getting up in the morning.

It's always good to reinforce the idea that you're in it for the long haul.

THE SQUEAKY WHEEL

"Ms. Jones, I trusted your company to provide quality service. That hasn't happened. What you don't know is that I can be an incredibly squeaky wheel. I've got a lot of time on my hands, and a justice streak a mile long. If we don't come to a resolution by this afternoon, I'm going to make sure that as many people as possible know that you don't take care of your customers. You're a smart businessperson, so here's a cost-benefit problem for you. How many of your potential customers have to go elsewhere before ignoring me becomes a losing proposition?"

"The Squeaky Wheel" more clearly states the business proposition and unmistakably affirms your status as a "justice seeker" with an empty calendar. Once again, you're not actually committing yourself to launching a year-long information campaign: your opponent only has to believe that you are willing and able to do it. Calling her a "smart businessperson" is a little flattery to give her a way out while saving face. The last line restates the situation as clearly as possible, just in case she's missed the point.

As I demonstrated in the first Unscrewed True Story, "The Unscrupulous Car Dealer," it's important to lay out the mathematics.

A HANDFUL OF SATURDAYS

"Mr. Smith…I'll bet that, in just a handful of Saturdays, I can convince a couple of dozen people to shop elsewhere. It could end up that, by not paying me what's due me, you lose ten times as much in future business. It won't put any cash in my pocket, but I'll feel a lot better about things. What do you think?"

I like the phrase "a handful of Saturdays," because the wording is a very soft sell. However, this presentation, like "doing my civic duty," adds in an important element: the notion that I may be just a little bit crazy and that I am willing to take action whether or not I get anything in return.

I've been asked, "Isn't The Unscrewed Promise a contradiction of The Unscrewed Purpose—that we're not trying to get even or gain revenge?" The answer is no.

You know what your purpose is, and what your goal is. What you say to your opponent may not have anything to do with your real objective. In the case of the shady car dealer, actually standing on the sidewalk in front of the car dealership handing out flyers might have never gained me a nickel. What turned the tide of the negotiations was the fact that the sales manager *completely believed* that I would keep up with my personal crusade until hell froze over or he found some way to satisfy me. His belief in my determination caused him to make the wise business decision to grant me the advertised discount on the car. If he had not been convinced that I was dedicated enough—and crazy enough—to pound the pavement for an indefinite period, he wouldn't have budged.

Sometimes the situation calls for you to go that extra inch—into (seemingly) certifiably crazy.

JUST A LITTLE BIT JACK

"As I see it, Bob, you and I have a disagreement here. You don't want to do what's right. I think you should. I know you're a busy man and that I might not seem that important to you. But you know what? Since my operation, I've had far too much time on my hands. My wife's been saying I need a hobby. You know what, Bob? *You* can become my hobby. I can spend my days standing in front of your store, performing a legitimate community service by telling folks just how you've treated me. Hell, I could use one of those little hand clickers to count how many unsuspecting souls I actually save from your regrettably destructive business practices. My doctor told me that fresh air would be good for me. What do you think, Bob? Do you want to become my hobby?"

Okay, I admit that to pull off "Just a Little Bit Jack," you've really got to have a little Jack Nicholson in you. But remember that nobody wants to become someone else's hobby. If you can dig deep and muster up a muse from *One Flew Over the Cuckoo's Nest*, the results can be instantaneous.

Despite the apparent lunacy, nowhere in the Promise can there be a threat to property or person. Those are deal breakers: "Do not pass Go. Do not collect $200."

The primary objective of the Promise is to convince your opponent that you are not going to go away, and that you are going to use up his or her time, effort, and energy in immense amounts if you do not get what you're asking for. Wording aside, the only real consideration on the table is how your "free speech" efforts are going to affect their bottom line.

Of course, the next question from your opponent will be, "How do you expect to do that?" In many cases, the Promise is just the opening volley. It puts your opponent on notice, so that when you explain or unleash your Unscrewed Plan, he or she will understand what is happening and why.

Some people have asked, "Aren't you just bluffing? What if someone calls your bluff?"

Although the ideal situation is that you not set foot on a sidewalk with a sign, once in a while you may end up doing it—for about ten minutes. Your opponent pretty quickly figures out the math. If you turn away just one customer, you've likely cost your opponent more than making things right with you.

The next story demonstrates the persuasive power of The Unscrewed Promise.

UNSCREWED TRUE STORY
The Remodeling Contractor

After thinking about it for several years, my wife and I decided it was finally time to add a formal dining room to one corner of our home. It was going to be a beautiful room, looking out onto a Western Oregon fir forest. We were experienced home remodelers, having already lived through a half-dozen projects. Therefore, because this project involved no plumbing or other complex infrastructure, we knew it should be relatively straightforward and trouble free.

We started the project in early August, with the understanding that it would be completed by Halloween. That was fine with us. The only thing that my wife was firm about was that it had to be finished by Thanksgiving.

Murphy's Law of assumptions almost immediately reared its ugly head. Not too long into the project, things started to go wrong. I'd call it a comedy of errors, except that it wasn't funny.

The new walls were built to the wrong thickness— four inches, rather than six inches. So the framers tore down the walls they had just put up. It could have been prevented if someone had taken a tape measure to any of the existing walls, which were—you guessed it—six inches. Moreover, these were the same people who had worked on the house for most of the preceding four years.

All the wall and window trim was stained, when it didn't need to be. All anyone needed to do was look at any of the other forty-four windows in the house to see what they should have looked like. They tried to sand the stain away. It didn't work, though they did succeed in covering the rest of the house with a layer of sawdust.

The foreman ordered the wrong mounting frames for the windows, which would cause a four-week delay in completing a two-month project.

Two attempts at stripping the stain from the window trim involved chemicals so foul that we were twice driven out of our home.

The floor was two inches too high. To remedy this, the carpenters cut up the floor and shaved the joists.

Painters painted the new dining room the wrong color, and then retouched the adjacent living room with the same wrong color, creating blotches all over the vaulted ceilings. The painting company owner showed up and denied that the color was a problem. "The paint just isn't dry yet," he said. Two days later, the color was still wrong.

The foreman we had worked with for years had lost control of the job site. The contractor, who had completed the six previous projects, was totally nonresponsive. The subcontractors weren't taking responsibility. We were already a month behind on the project. Thanksgiving in the new dining room would have to wait a year. As things were going, our holiday season would be augmented by the sound of nail guns and the smell of curing paint. My wife was about to shoot someone—possibly me.

Something had to be done.

I called the general contractor, Steve, and told him that he wouldn't get paid one more cent unless he and his entire team, including subcontractors, showed up on the job site at nine the following morning.

He said that he wasn't sure whether he could get everyone together that quickly. I said, "Well, I am sure…that you want to get paid someday. If you and your team aren't here tomorrow morning, that day might be a long way off."

One of the myths about contractors is that, at the drop of a hat, they can put a lien on your home that will ruin your credit rating and everything else financial. In most jurisdictions, a lien matters only if you plan to sell your house. Our general contractor was aware that this was our "twenty-five-year" family home and therefore, threatening to place a lien on the property would have little effect. He didn't even bother to bring it up.

I went upstairs to my office, logged onto the Internet, and found what I was looking for. A half hour later, I put two sheets of paper into a manila folder and went downstairs for dinner.

The general contractor arrived promptly at nine the next morning and assured me the rest of the team would be there soon. He was really the only one I needed to talk to, though having the subcontractors present would help bring things to a quicker conclusion. The foreman drove up ten minutes later. We waited a half hour for the painting contractor to stumble up to the front door. "I rolled my truck off the driveway," he said. A cynical person might think that he had crashed his truck into the gully to gain sympathy. I didn't give him that much credit.

After we were all assembled, I ran through the list of screwups to that point. The foreman and painting contractor pulled out pocketfuls of excuses and justifications. The general contractor supported his team. So far, things had progressed exactly as I'd expected.

While the foreman and the painting contractor inspected the ceiling blotches in the living room, I took the general contractor into the kitchen.

"Would you like a cup of coffee?" I asked.

"Yes. That would be nice. Black, please."

"Of course."

As I handed him his cup, I said, "I need this project finished by the middle of December."

"That's not possible," he replied. "We've got a lot of other projects going on. I can't spare the people. We're going to run into January. I'm sorry."

This was the man who had shaken my hand and assured me that the project would be completed by the end of October.

"I'm sorry, too, Steve. That's not good enough. I've talked with one of your competitors. He is prepared to bring his team in here this afternoon and will guarantee in writing to have the job finished by my deadline. I am also so disappointed in your performance here that I feel obligated to warn other homeowners about this fiasco."

Steve wrapped both hands around the cup, as if looking for warmth in a room that had suddenly turned very cold.

"What do you mean by that?"

I opened the manila folder and removed both sheets of paper. I laid them side by side on the kitchen counter.

On the left was the advertising rate sheet for the daily newspaper.

On the right was a quarter-page print ad I had created on my computer. The headline was a single-word question: "Remodeling?" Below that was the name of the contracting company inside a red circle with a line through it—the international symbol for "no." And below that were my name and phone number with the plea, "Call Me for ABC Construction Horror Stories!" For $10 I had snagged the web site name www.dontgowithABCconstruction.com and added that to the advertisement. At the bottom of the ad was the line, "More ABC Construction Horror Stories Wanted."

Steve clutched the coffee cup. "Would you really run this?" he asked.

I looked him straight in the eye. "You bet."

"I thought that after all this time, we were friends."

"Friends would have showed concern when my family was forced to move out of our house for the second time in two months because of your screwups."

I refilled my own cup of coffee and then added some half-and-half. "The bottom line, Steve, is that we need our house back. You need to complete the job by the middle of the month, or else this ad will be in section A of the daily paper."

Steve looked pale.

"If you'll notice," I said, pointing to the newspaper rate card, "there's a nice price break for a week-long run."

Steve picked up the ad. He stared at it for almost a minute. "Nice work," he said dryly.

"Thank you," I replied. "Are you going to finish the project by the fifteenth, or do I call in the other guys?"

"We'll get it done," he said.

"You understand, I'm not going to pay one more cent on this project until it is completed?"

"Of course," he said.

We shook hands. He spoke for a few minutes with his foreman and the painting contractor. That afternoon, a pair of carpenters arrived to finish the detail work. At the crack of dawn the following morning, four painters appeared at the front door.

The work was completed on December 14, and the Burley family enjoyed a wonderful holiday dinner in their new dining room.

THE UNSCREWED
POWER TOOLS

The Unscrewed Power Tools are five technologies and one nontechnical method that you use to leverage your position with your opponent.

You have weapons in your arsenal that you will use to change the mind of a businessperson who has decided that you aren't worth his or her time or attention. These Power Tools are as follows:

- telephone
- fax machine
- computer and printer
- Internet
- e-mail
- personal visit

As with any tools, their effectiveness depends on the ability and knowledge of the handler. Used properly, these Power Tools can overcome any objection, are versatile enough to sidestep any obstacle, and are strong enough to tire even the most obstinate opponent.

You use telephones and fax machines to reach deep within the heart of the corporate beast.

Your computer is the creativity engine that takes your ideas and, with the assistance of your printer, turns them into powerful messages of change.

The Internet gives you access to vast amounts of useful information.

E-mail gives you the ability to spread your message far and wide, denying refuge for the offending company.

A personal visit is a well-planned and well-executed frontal assault on the fundamental assumptions of the corrupt business mind.

Let's take a brief look at each of the tools and how they are used.

TELEPHONE

Your telephone is the most powerful weapon in your arsenal. In these days of cell phones and satellite phones, we sometimes take for granted the incredible ability of this device: with it, you can instantaneously reach halfway around the world.

Of course, telephones can also be a hassle. Solicitation calls are an irritation. I'm sure that you have placed your number on the "Do Not Call" list by now.

But you know what? Companies never put themselves on the "Do Not Call" list. They depend on getting calls. It's their business to receive calls. That means they are there, every business day, waiting for you to dial their number. If that number is the CEO's inside line, then all you need to know is exactly what to say.

What do you say? By the time you finish this book, you will know the precise words you need to accomplish your goal.

FAX MACHINE

Some historians have argued that the fax machine—not television, radio, or even e-mail—is the most important communication tool invented in the past 100 years.

I'm not sure I'd go that far, but faxing does have some very special qualities.

The fax machine combines the instantaneous communication of the telephone with the power of the written word. A fax document can be legally binding, even though it is just a picture of the original.

You won't use the fax machine as a terrorist tool—sending a thousand faxes just to "burn up their toner." That's the fax equivalent of a computer virus: annoying, but purposeless.

You'll use the almost magical ability of the fax machine to create something tangible: a printed page. When that sheet of paper slides out of the fax machine, it is difficult to ignore. Unlike e-mail, it cannot be deleted, unseen, with the tap of a key. Even if it's tossed in the trash can, someone must read enough of it to see what it is.

Most magical of all, the same message can be sent to dozens of different places automatically and nearly simultaneously—with dozens of different pairs of hands and eyes forced to handle and read whatever you send them.

COMPUTER AND PRINTER

Of course, your computer is the platform for creativity, publication, research, writing, calculating, access to the Internet, and e-mail. It will also be the nerve center for most of your Unscrewed activities. What you might not know is that your computer is likely able to do a few special tricks, such as automated telephone dialing and recording, automated faxing, and other automated tasks.

INTERNET

Many aspects of the Internet make it a powerful tool in your arsenal. It is an excellent tool for researching your adversary and the competition. Internet chat rooms and forums can give insight into the workings of the company and how they deal with customer complaints. Internet search engines are a powerful tool for helping you locate unpublished telephone and fax numbers.

E-MAIL

Just a few years ago, e-mail had the potential to be the most important Unscrewed technological tool of all. In the past few years, however, the amount of unwanted e-mail, or spam, has grown exponentially. Companies used to routinely publicize their internal e-mail addresses. Today, that is rare. In addition, software security firms market programs that are very effec-

---

THE GROWTH OF SPAM

If you use e-mail, you've been a recipient of unsolicited e-mail, better known as spam.

The spam situation continues to worsen dramatically. In 2004, the market research firm International Data Corporation reported that spam accounted for 38 percent of all e-mail received in North America—up to 11 billion pieces of spam a day.

Incredibly, other industry watchers think those numbers are conservative. In May 2004, the spam fighters at Brightmail, Inc. (now part of Symantec), calculated that spam accounted for 64 percent of all e-mail, with 86 percent of the electronic garbage originating in the United States.

Dealing with spam infestation costs U.S. companies $2,000 to $4,000 annually *per employee*. Adding insult to injury, as it gobbles up bandwidth, spam slows down everything else on the Internet.

Numerous federal agencies—from the FBI to the Interstate Commerce Commission—have joined the antispam battle. Congress passed antispam legislation. The U.S. attorney general and several states have successfully prosecuted several of the worst spammers. Much of the remaining spam community left the jurisdiction. They moved their operations overseas, beyond the long arm of the U.S. law.

More than anything else, spam has limited the usefulness of e-mail for Unscrewers—and everyone else.

tive in filtering out unwanted or unsolicited e-mails, limiting e-mail's effectiveness as a tool to reach into companies.

Even if you do manage to get an e-mail inside a company, it is, unfortunately, easily dismissed and deleted.

But e-mail is not entirely useless. Anyone who's ever received an e-mail chain letter recognizes that. E-mail remains a powerful tool for spreading a message among already associated users. It is this aspect of e-mail that you can leverage.

PERSONAL VISIT

The idea of walking into a place of business and speaking directly with a recalcitrant manager or owner is scary to a lot of people. It needn't be. As you read in the Unscrewed True Story about my wife's experience with Blue State Tires ("The Bait-and-Switch Tire Store"), a personal visit is a way to get your point across quickly.

Sometimes you don't even have to implement your strategy: just showing up is enough. Recently, an attorney friend of mine told a friend of his with consumer woes the tire store story. Inspired, the mistreated consumer carried a folder full of flyers into a car dealership that had been giving her a hard time about a "lemon" they had sold her. Just having that manila folder under her arm gave her the courage to confront the dealership and not take no for an answer. The upshot? They relented. (And she didn't even have to open the folder.)

Sometimes it takes a while to figure out which strategy to use in a particular situation. Other times, a company leaves the door wide open for you, as was the case in the next story.

UNSCREWED TRUE STORY

The Printer Maker

In the summer of 2002, I spent more than $400 on one of those high-end digital photo printers from an online retailer that I'll call Volga. I unpacked it and hooked it up to my Windows 98 PC. It worked great. The special paper was kind of expensive, except in bulk. Knowing that I'd be using a lot of it, I bought a case for more than $200. I was more than $600 into the project, but happy with the results. The only problem was that it took a long time for each picture to pop out of the machine. After a while, I realized that my Microsoft Windows 98 machine was the problem: it was a few years old, with a slow processor and not enough memory.

After a few months of tedium, I finally got fed up waiting for the pictures to pop out. It didn't seem right to buy a new computer just to speed up a snapshot printer. But I rationalized it by telling myself that a new PC would speed up everything else I did, and that would make it worth the investment.

I drove out to my local "big-box" computer retailer and bought a brand-new, superfast, multimedia, giga-RAM–equipped, graphics-enhanced Windows XP computer. I spent an entire afternoon and evening setting up the new system. I copied files from the old PC to the new one. The grandfather clock in the dining room chimed ten as I turned off the power on the old system for the final time. One last thing to do: hook up the photo printer. It was already late, but that was really why I'd gotten the new computer in the first place. I wasn't about to go to bed without seeing at least one picture fly out of the new system.

I set the photo printer on the desk next to the monitor. I dutifully turned everything off before hooking it up. After checking the connections, I turned the PC back on. The light glowed green, the hard drive whirred, the Windows logo appeared, and the "Found new hardware" message appeared. So far, so good. A message box asked me to locate the "driver" for the new device—the photo printer. A driver is a small software program that lets a device—in this case, a printer—"talk" with the computer. I found the installation CD that came with the photo printer and inserted it into the CD drive. A new message box popped up: "This driver is not compatible with Windows XP."

I searched the CD files for another driver. No luck. I searched the Internet for an update. Apparently, none existed. Near midnight, I gave up, frustrated but still hopeful. I'd call Tech Support in the morning. They would certainly have the answer.

Just after eight in the morning, I was again perched on the chair at my desk, cup of coffee in one hand, phone in the other. A recorded voice told me that my "expected wait will be twenty-three minutes." Just less than a half hour later, a human finally appeared on the other end of the line. I quickly explained the situation and waited for instructions on how I could get the XP printer driver.

"You can't," Mark—Tech Support agent number 24050—said.

"What do you mean?" I asked.

"There isn't one," he replied.

"That can't be."

"Believe me, it's true."

"But I've had the printer for only a few months. And Windows XP has been around for *more than a year*. (Bill Gates launched Windows XP with great fanfare in New York on October 25, 2001, with Mayor Rudolph Giuliani by his side.) Are you telling me that even if I had bought my new computer and the printer at the same time, they wouldn't have worked together?"

"That's right."

I still wasn't sure that I had the story right. "Are you telling me that your company was selling a $400 photo printer that was incompatible with the latest operating system available at the time?"

"That's right."

"Are you also telling me that your company has no intention of ever creating an XP-compatible driver for my printer?"

"That's right."
"No, it isn't."
Something had to be done.

I gave Mark a chance to make things right.

"Mark, as PC power users, you and I both know that it isn't right to be selling a Windows PC accessory that is incompatible with the latest version of Windows out there. Here's your chance to be a hero."

"What do you mean?"

"I'd like a refund for the printer, and for what remains of the case of photo paper I also purchased."

"Yeah, I know you're right. But I can't do that. They don't let me handle the money. You'll have to talk with Customer Service. I can connect you."

The customer service agent wasn't any help. It took me fifteen minutes just to get her to understand the problem. It was wasted time. "It's not our policy to give refunds on products purchased from our retailers."

I called the online retailer. They apologized, but said that there was nothing they could do. I was well outside their thirty-day return period. They did suggest that if the printer was broken, it could be returned to the manufacturer for a new one—with the same problem.

Convinced that the printer manufacturer wasn't ever going to upgrade the unit so it would run with my new computer, I went back to the store that sold me the computer and purchased a different photo printer from a different manufacturer that was guaranteed to be compatible with Windows XP. So although I was back in the photo business, I hadn't solved my original problem: getting my money back for the first printer.

A few months earlier, I'd come up with a new version of the "standing on the street corner" approach to remedying a consumer problem, and I'd been wanting to try it. It had the potential to reach a much larger group of would-be customers.

A web site feature that Volga had pioneered was online customer product reviews. They were posted on the same page as the product information. I'd wondered what would happen if a customer reported a faulty product or poor customer service in a review. I imagined several possibilities. The review could be rejected. It could be ignored. Or…someone just might pay attention to it.

It took me a few days to get around to writing the review. I posted it on the Volga site, and then went downstairs to grab some lunch. I was almost finished with my peanut butter–and–banana sandwich when the phone rang. The caller ID displayed the name of the printer maker.

"Mr. Burley," said a melodious voice on the other end, "my name is Vicki, and I'm a senior supervisor in the Customer Service Department."

"Hey, Vithee," I said with difficulty. (I really needed a glass of milk to wash down the last of my sandwich.) "What'h goin' on."

"Mr. Burley, I am calling to follow up on the call you had earlier with one of our agents. You're a loyal customer of ours, and we want to make sure that we do our best to resolve any outstanding issues."

Her sentence was long enough that I was able to pour and drink half a glass of moo juice. "That's great," I said, noting that she was aware that I owned other products of theirs. I hadn't mentioned that to the first customer service representative, so she must have read it in the online review.

"I see that you've been having a problem with your photo printer and Windows XP. As you are aware, we are not going to be updating the driver for that particular model. What I'd like to offer you is an exchange for one of our newer models. Would that be satisfactory?"

"No, I don't think so," I replied.

"Well, what would you consider fair?" Vicki asked.

"Considering you purposely marketed an obsolete item, I think it's only appropriate that you give me a complete refund for the printer and the photo paper."

"By the way, Mr. Burley, where did you purchase the unit?" Even though I was pretty sure she already knew, I told her.

"Did you use a credit card?"

"Yes."

She asked if she could put me on hold for "a minute." I usually don't like to be put on hold, but in this case, I thought it might be all right.

Vicki returned to the line in barely thirty seconds.

"Mr. Burley, it appears you were caught in the middle of a transition between models. The unit you purchased should not have been available at the time you ordered it. Therefore, my supervisor approved a full refund to your credit card. If you could fax us your original receipts or card statements, I'll make sure you get a prompt credit."

"Thank you. That would be wonderful," I said. "Where shall I ship the old one?"

"No need. We are no longer selling that model. You can keep it if you like."

"I'm not sure what I'll do with it, but thank you."

Once off the line, I faxed the receipts. Two days later, the credit had been applied to my online statement. The old photo printer ended up as a "because you're you" gift to my father-in-law, who will probably never upgrade his Windows 95 PC.

To this day, the printer maker has never upgraded the driver. Strangely, they never asked me to revise or withdraw the online review. You can still view it. Just type the following into any Internet search engine: ron burley photo printer review.

I was also pleased to add the "online street corner" technique to the Unscrewed tool kit.

THE UNSCREWED PLAN

The Unscrewed Plan is designed to recover what you are due; it includes an acceptable goal, adversary research, a specific strategy, a realistic timeline, and an honest assessment of the situation.

The Unscrewed Plan is at once your checklist, guidebook, and script. (It's also your road map. And your cheat sheet.) Once you have been dismissed by Customer Service and decided that you're in need of an Unscrewing, the first thing you do is create your plan of action.

The plan has five steps:

1. Set an acceptable goal.
2. Research your adversary.
3. Select a specific strategy.
4. Create a realistic timeline.
5. Make an honest assessment of the situation.

At times, each of these items may be only a sentence or two. In more complex situations or where more is at stake, your plan may run into several pages.

To begin with, I recommend actually writing out the plan, so that you can hold it in your hand, refer to it, and make notes while you're in the middle of the Unscrewing process. Once you're an accomplished Unscrewer, you'll have no problem going through the whole process in your head.

SET AN ACCEPTABLE GOAL

At first glance, your goal might seem obvious: it's the dollar amount you're so angry about. However, your acceptable goal is not necessarily to reclaim the same amount of money or value that you've been cheated out of. Your goal should take into account everything you have lost, balanced against a realistic estimation of what you think you can get.

On the upside, you can add in anything that is directly related to the loss and for which you can show a bill or receipt: long-distance phone calls, notary or legal fees, shipping costs, and so on.

Here is an example. Your bank mistakenly bounces a deposited check—they misread the endorsement. This causes several checks you've written to bounce, repeatedly. You incur multiple bounced-check fees at your bank and are charged additional fees from the companies that received your checks. Your mortgage company adds an additional one-half percent to your rate to cover mortgage insurance added because of your poor credit.

You'll remember how I handled a similar situation in an earlier Unscrewed True Story, "The UnPayroll Company." Our company received payment of all fees, plus additional compensation and actions. In this situation, an acceptable goal would include complete compensation for all fees and a letter from the bank to the mortgage company, explaining that the error was theirs. This is actually the most important part of the goal. *A one-half percent interest bump on a typical thirty-year mortgage for a family home would increase total payments by more than $10,000.* That fact makes the letter from the mortgage company the most valuable component of the compensation package.

Most of the time, you will attempt to be fully compensated for your loss. However, in some circumstances, it may be obvious that is not possible. When a company has gone out of business or has filed for bankruptcy, nonsecured creditors are usually at the back of the repayment line. However, as the old saying goes, "Something is better than nothing." If a company is on the ropes and you are willing to revise your acceptable goal to something less than your actual damages, you may find that you can come to an immediate agreement for a lesser amount. You will assess your adversary in the next step.

Even though my time is valuable, I never try to get a company to compensate me directly for the time I spend in getting them to do what they should. I might try to fit the value of that time into some other category, though you shouldn't expect to be compensated for your "collection" effort. Although it may seem reasonable, compensation for personal time is rarely considered, even in court cases. In the get-in-and-get-out strategy of The Unscrewed Solution, it is an unnecessary distraction, and I guarantee that you would spend more time arguing about it than it was worth.

Once you have decided on an acceptable goal, write it down and do not deviate from it, unless your research directs you to do so. In that case, revise it accordingly—and then stick to it.

RESEARCH YOUR ADVERSARY

The Internet is, by far, the best way to research any company. You do not need to pay for reports from professional financial research companies. I usually find all the information I need about a company in less than fifteen minutes online.

The key questions you want to answer about your adversary are as follows:

1. Who are the principal players in the corporation: chief executive officer, president, vice president of sales, vice president of customer relations, and vice president of investor relations? Many companies post online biographies of their principals. Read them. You never know what little piece of information might be helpful. You might learn that you and the CEO attended the same college, support the same charities, or share a passion for full-contact shuffleboard.

2. Where is the corporate headquarters? It's always nice if the HQ is right down the street—meaning within 100

miles. The last thing they want is an unsatisfied customer showing up and creating a scene in their staid corporate environs. On the other hand, even if the HQ isn't down the street, the information can be helpful. "I'm going to be visiting my cousin in Atlanta next Monday, and will make sure I stop by to chat with your CEO about this."

3. What are the phone numbers, fax numbers, and e-mail addresses for the headquarters, principals, Investor Relations Department, and Sales Department? As you've read so far in the Unscrewed True Stories, these are your keys to the castle. Although the main contact information for the company may be listed on the web page, contact information for the individual principals can be difficult to find. I recommend using the Google Internet search engine. Enter the name of each of the principals and the word "phone." It would look like this, including the quotation marks: "Bill Gates" "CEO Microsoft phone:"—note the colon after "phone." This is the way it would likely appear on a web page. Internet search engines are very literal. Search the same way for fax and e-mail addresses. You may also find the information listed in noncorporate sources. I once found a CEO's private fax number listed in the minutes of a charity meeting. He was a member of the board of directors and had given it out during the meeting. Sometimes the easiest way into a company is through the Sales Department or Investor Relations Department. These numbers are often listed on the company web site. We will discuss how to deal with each of these offices and individuals in a later chapter. "But I'm not an investor," you say. "Not yet," I reply.

4. Is it a public company that issues stock, or is it privately held? Several of the Unscrewed techniques leverage the legal requirements of publicly traded companies. Privately held companies, on the other hand, are immune to those techniques: we have other ways of convincing them to see the light.

5. Does the company have physical offices or retail outlets in your state? If you made a purchase online, you may have more options if it has a physical presence in your state.

6. What are the annual revenues? If a company is publicly traded, you can find out most financial information by going to the Yahoo! financial pages and entering the company's stock symbol. If you do not know the stock symbol, find it by entering the company's name or part of the company's name. The financial pages will contain more information than you could possibly need for your efforts. The main numbers you are looking for are annual revenues, quarterly and annual profits, and current stock price. This information is not available for privately held companies that do not issue stock.

7. Who are the competitors? Knowing who the company butts heads with is valuable in several of the Unscrewed techniques. For example, you saw the powerful effect using that knowledge had in the Unscrewed True Story "The Bait-and-Switch Tire Store." Many times, the information is obvious. For large corporations, a list of competitors can often be found in free online investment research sites, such as CBS MarketWatch or Yahoo! Finance.

8. Is the company regulated or monitored by a government agency? If so, which agency of local, state, or federal government? Hard-wire telephone companies and other utilities are regulated in many jurisdictions by the Public Utilities Commission. Any company using electronic transmission—cell phone company, satellite or WiFi provider—falls under the jurisdiction of the Federal Communications Commission (FCC). Airlines are regulated by the Federal Aviation Administration (FAA) and National Transportation Safety Board (NTSB). All other modes of public transportation fall under the NTSB, though waterborne craft are also overseen by the United States Coast Guard. Food service establishments and food product manufacturers are subject to local, county, state, and federal standards. For public corporations, much of

this information can be gleaned from public filings on financial web sites. You don't need to know every regulatory agency that deals with your adversary. However, it can be helpful in discussions for the company to know that you know who holds the leash on its continued ability to do business. As you'll recall from the Unscrewed True Story "The Telephone Installation Nightmare," my friend Jack made good use of this information when he promised to show up at every Public Utility Commission meeting for the next decade unless his phone lines were fixed.

Write down your research answers. You don't have to take lengthy notes, but a few jotted reminders of who's who and what's what will greatly help you during your discussions. We're not lawyers. We're not going to argue details. We're just trying to figure out who we're dealing with, how to get in touch with the people who can make the decision to help us, and what may be important to them. Sometimes information reveals itself as important only because it is written down.

SELECT A SPECIFIC STRATEGY
After researching your adversary, you will need to decide the best way to exercise The Unscrewed Principle, and present The Unscrewed Promise in that particular situation.

In each Unscrewed True Story, you've read about the techniques that can be used, and how effective they can be. In the following chapters, we will discuss more than a dozen different techniques you will be able to use to get your way. You will combine one or more of these techniques with your research to develop a strategy that will give you the best chance of achieving your goal in the least amount of time.

CREATE A REALISTIC TIMELINE
The Unscrewed timeline consists of the following:

- Your timeline to implement the plan. This includes when you will start, a checklist, and a deadline for things that need to get done—such as calling financial institutions to assess credit damage or making a run to a copy shop to photocopy flyers.

- The deadline you will state to your adversary. When you are at the point in your negotiation when you make your promise, it is important that you are specific about your expectations—not only about what you expect, but also when you expect it.

With "The Unscrupulous Car Dealer," it was immediate. Mitch at "The Bait-and-Switch Tire Store" understood that he had to put different tires on Hali's SUV before I walked out the door. Jack ("The Telephone Installation Nightmare") told his phone company: "today." With "The Remodeling Contractor," all that really mattered was that *he* was there to see my creations. The foreman and the painters were only props and a nice audience. I could have dived right into the conversation when the contractor arrived; however, waiting for the audience helped him make the decision faster. If you fail to provide a deadline, there is no pressure on your adversary.

Write down your deadline and repeat it to yourself. Once you do that, it will be much easier to say it when the time comes. Make a decision about your satisfaction timeline—and stick to it.

You don't need to be extremely detailed about the timeline. Often, a few key milestones will do just fine.

In the final step, in which you assess the situation, your timeline will give you an idea of the time commitment needed to implement your strategy. If it will take too long, the goal might not be worth the effort.

MAKE AN HONEST ASSESSMENT OF THE SITUATION

The final item in every Unscrewed Plan is an assessment. You need to answer one question: Is reclaiming the monetary value of this loss worth my time and effort?

You may not have given a lot of thought to the nonwork hourly value of your time. This is not the equivalent of how much you get paid at your job, because we're talking about free time or quality time—time taken out of relaxation and play hours. Free time is much more valuable than what you get paid for your job. Double what you earn working to get the value of your free time, which we'll call your Unscrewed pay rate.

If you get paid by the hour, just double your hourly rate to get your Unscrewed rate.

If you're not an hourly wage earner—such as a salaried employee, contract worker, or consultant—figure roughly $5 per hour for every $10,000 per year in gross earnings. (See the chart that follows.) Therefore, if you earn $60,000 per year, your gross hourly rate is $30 per hour. Your Unscrewed rate is $60 per hour.

That means that if you've been ripped off for $300, you shouldn't plan on spending more than five hours getting yourself Unscrewed. Anything more than that wouldn't be worth your time. Even at that, if you count your time against what you will have recovered, you've still only broken even. That's why we want to regain as much as is morally acceptable while taking as little time as possible to get it.

SALARY TO HOURLY CONVERSION

Annual Salary	Hourly Equivalent	Unscrewed Value
$10,000	$5.00	$10.00
$15,000	$7.50	$15.00
$20,000	$10.00	$20.00
$25,000	$12.50	$25.00
$30,000	$15.00	$30.00
$35,000	$17.50	$35.00
$40,000	$20.00	$40.00
$45,000	$22.50	$45.00
$50,000	$25.00	$50.00
$55,000	$27.50	$55.00
$60,000	$30.00	$60.00

$65,000	$32.50	$65.00
$70,000	$35.00	$70.00
$75,000	$37.50	$75.00
$80,000	$40.00	$80.00
$85,000	$42.50	$85.00
$90,000	$45.00	$90.00
$95,000	$47.50	$95.00
$100,000	$50.00	$100.00

The final task of the assessment is setting that decision point when you should throw in the towel. At that point, you have either invested more time and effort than the situation is worth, or you can see that recovering what you are due will cost you more—in time, money, and effort—than it is worth. If you design your plan properly, you are unlikely to reach this point. However, if you do, you will probably be even more frustrated and angry than when you started, because you have invested a great deal but must walk away empty-handed.

No matter how angry you are about getting ripped off, if getting what you deserve is going to cost you more than it's worth, forget about it and move on. This is a difficult truth to accept. You have to know when getting Unscrewed is worth your time and when it isn't, and act accordingly. Don't spend a day chasing 75¢ lost in a soda machine. On the other hand, if you've been taken for several thousand dollars by an unscrupulous contractor, you have a good justification for investing considerable time and effort in recovering the loss.

If you earn $60,000 a year in salary, a $2,000 loss would be worth almost thirty-five hours of Unscrewed time. The good news is, most of the Unscrewed techniques take less than an hour, so your rate of return on that time invested would be an astounding $2,000 per hour!

The Unscrewed Solution works in almost all situations—except when it doesn't. In my experience, it fails only when you, or your adversary, decide to make the situation personal, rather than financial. That is why you should be very careful never to make personal attacks. Once the battle becomes personal, you will lose. (Except when the situation needs to be approached in a personal way. More about that in chapter 14, "Three Techniques for Dealing with the Government and Megacorporations.")

The importance of choosing the right technique cannot be understated. It's the equivalent of choosing the right weapon when going into battle. And, as the next story demonstrates, when you make the right choice, the results can be amazing.

UNSCREWED TRUE STORY
The Uncommunicative Cell Phone Company

I have to be honest with you. There were some situations that, for a long time, I just couldn't figure out how to Unscrew reliably. The most difficult situation was dealing with a large corporation with whom I did a small amount of business on a regular basis, such as the garbage collection company or cable TV provider. My monthly bill could be as high as $50. However, even if they triple-billed me, I'd be out only $150.

Most disturbing, these were the companies that most often hid behind voice mail mazes and e-mail walls. I had to figure out a way to get the attention of the company quickly and have it resolve the situation almost instantaneously. For years, I decided that many of these small losses weren't worth the time I'd have to spend chasing them, even though I hated letting the companies get away with nickel-and-diming me.

I was sitting in church one Sunday when I finally figured it out. It wasn't a signal from the Almighty. My epiphany was actually inspired by a moment in the service when congregants have an opportunity to share their thoughts at an open microphone.

I sat on the idea for a few months, waiting for just the right situation to try out my theory. It appeared when my friend Tonya called me one spring afternoon. Her cell phone company had been jerking her around for several months over a $200 billing error.

Something had to be done.

I got the particulars on the situation from Tonya and told her I'd have it straightened out within a couple of hours.

"I've been talking with them for months," she said. "Good luck!" (Tonya is a slightly cynical former New Yorker.)

I sat down at my computer and typed in the company name: Universal Cellular. I quickly scanned its web site and found the information I was looking for, which was a link to the Investor Relations page and the stock symbol.

I clicked over to my stockbroker's web site, logged into my account, and purchased ten shares of Universal Cellular Corporation (UCC) for about $60. There I was, a proud stockholder, an owner in the company that had been giving my friend such a hard time.

I picked up the phone and called the UCC Investor Relations Department. A very pleasant-voiced woman answered the phone.

"UCC Investor Relations. This is Felicia. How can I help you?"

I introduced myself and then let her know the reason I was calling. "As an active UCC stockholder, I am concerned that we treat our customers fairly."

"We do our best," she assured me, sounding as though she were an agent at a first-class ticket counter.

I filled her in on the whole story, and concluded, "I was appalled when Tonya told me the problems she's had with a simple billing dispute." We were two minutes into the conversation. Total time invested thus far: seven minutes.

"I'm very sorry, Mr. Burley. I assure you, we value every member of the UCC family, whether customer, employee, or stockholder."

"I'm sure you do, Felicia. However, this has upset me so much that I have decided not to vote by proxy this year. I want to exercise my right as a stockholder to show up at our annual meeting, stand at the microphone, and let the chair of the board, Mr. Henson, know about this problem. I mean, if we can't—"

Felicia cut me off.

"Mr. Burley, I'm sure that won't be necessary," she said nervously. "If you can just give me Tonya's information, I'm sure we can straighten this out in no time. Is there a number I can reach you at in a few minutes?"

I gave her the number and hung up. Total time invested: nine minutes. This was what I had hoped for. My epiphany had been that no one in an Investor Relations Department wants some pissed-off minor stockholder screwing up the company's well-choreographed annual meeting. If some whining nobody scared an analyst or two into thinking that UCC's customers were less than happy, it could have a dele-terious effect on the stock price. Even a 1¢ dip in the quote could mean a $1,000,000 loss in market capitalization.

I actually received the good news via e-mail from Tonya a minute or so before Felicia called me back.

"Your friend has been taken care of, Mr. Burley. Thank you for bringing this to our attention."

"You're welcome," I said. "Whether employee or stock-holder, we all have to do our part to make sure that UCC is the best company it can be, right?"

"Absolutely," she said. "Thank you."

I hung up the phone and logged back into my brokerage account. UCC was up 60¢ on the day. I sold the ten shares, banking a clean $6 in the process (my brokerage doesn't charge commissions on individual trades).

Total return: $206.

Total time: ten minutes.

That put my Unscrewed pay rate at a generous $1,236 per hour.

Not too bad. I was a little sad, though. I was sure I would miss being a valued member of the UCC family.

ANATOMY OF A
TELEPHONE CALL

Most Unscrewed negotiations take place over the telephone. In this chapter, we'll cover the do's and don'ts of telephone negotiations. Many of the principles will apply to in-person visits as well, and we'll cover those in the next chapter.

Think of your telephone as an extension of your right arm, allowing you to reach out across thousands of miles, tap your adversary on the shoulder, and make the point that you're not going to go away. It is an extraordinarily powerful tool if used correctly. If used incorrectly, the telephone can also be the quickest way to guarantee that you will not get what you deserve.

The initial step of every Unscrewed Plan will be a courtesy call to Customer Service. It's only fair to give a company the chance to be one of the nine out of ten companies that still believes the customer is at least sometimes right. However, even before that first call, you will be preparing yourself for the possibility that things will not turn out well and that you may need to Unscrew the situation.

Most people call Customer Service feeling either apologetic for bringing a problem to their attention or indignant that their product or service is causing them a problem. Neither approach is effective. Before you even pick up the phone, there are a few basic rules of Unscrewed telephone etiquette that you need to know.

- Keep your cool. To be in control of the conversation, you must first be in control of yourself. Never yell, scream, shout, or otherwise raise your voice. Stay calm and businesslike. Have a smile in your voice. No matter what the other person says, do not get aggressive, pissy, sarcastic, patronizing, or saccharine. Speak in a calm, measured voice. Your words, rather than your tone, will get you what you want. As in the example Promise "Just a Little Bit Jack," sometimes the quietest voice is the most powerful. Remember this: the one who yells first, loses. I am speaking from experience. Early on in the development of the Unscrewed Solution, I tried all of it: yelling, threats, sarcasm, and so on. In time, I discovered that each of these behaviors gives your opponent an opportunity and a reason to dismiss you as a crackpot, loony, or otherwise less-than-credible individual.

- Keep it clean and civil. Just staying calm is not enough. Use pleasant, nonaggressive language. Your feelings may be hurt because the product or service failed, but the person on the other end of the line doesn't know you. His or her reluctance to help is no measure of your character. You are negotiating a business deal. There is nothing personal about it, in either direction. Never swear or slander. Never call someone a name or make a sexist or racist remark: the customer service representative has every right to hang up on you—and will. Above all, *never, ever* make physical threats to the person or the company. These are also instant disqualifiers, and you could end up with the police at your door. Once in a while, you may get lucky. Your opponent may be the one to lose his cool. If he calls you a "slime-dwelling son of a nocturnal reptile," you may have just hit the jackpot—particularly if you were taping the call.

- Stick to business. Avoid making personal comments, no matter how innocent they may seem (see the next

TAKING CONTROL OF THE CONVERSATION

Being in control means questioning every request and every action of your opponent every step of the way.

Don't Get Put on Hold

Representative: May I put you on hold?

You: No, you may not, Dave. You *can* put down your headset and go speak to your supervisor. I will wait right here on the line for you to return.

No Call-Backs

Representative: I need to speak with my supervisor about this. Can I take your number and call you right back?

You: I'll be happy to wait, Sara. I have nothing better to do right now than to make sure that you are today's customer service hero for XYZ Corporation.

Don't Waste Your Time

You: Steve, I know this problem is probably beyond your authority. Why don't we escalate it? (*Escalate* is customer service talk for "moving you up the food chain.") I'd like to talk with your supervisor. Can you connect me, please?

You don't want to waste time with someone who doesn't have the knowledge or authority to give you what you deserve. Notice that you're not slamming Steve's abilities, just recognizing the limits of his authority. At that point, he's probably more than happy to escalate the call. If you get the supervisor on the line, you will need to treat it as a brand-new call. Start right from the beginning: get the information, introduce yourself, state your problem, and present your acceptable resolution. If there is no supervisor and you're not making progress, that's the end of the courtesy call and time to get Unscrewed.

Unscrewed True Story, "The Unfriendly Skies"). Although it may seem as though it's a good idea to chitchat with the representative in order to build rapport, it could work against you. If you present yourself as Ms. Nice, it will be difficult later on to change into Ms. Maybe-Crazy.

- Take control of the conversation. Customer service people are quite skilled at dealing with calls. They expect you to do what they tell you: they expect you to obey. They are thrown off kilter by a quiet, determined, unrelenting caller. There's no page in their script for someone who refuses to go where they want them to. You want to be neither friend nor foe of the corporation or its representative. You are a business partner entering into a negotiation. Therefore, you want to be businesslike and resolute. You are the one in control of the conversation and the negotiation.

Making the mental leap from pleading consumer to business equal can take some practice. For most of our lives, we've been trained to be cattle led through a series of metal chutes to a destiny predetermined by outside forces.

The customer service representative is depending on you to follow the path that she wants to channel you into. If you do that, you will not get what you deserve. You will end up getting merely what she thinks is the minimum necessary for you to go away. Only by taking control of the situation, by making her go "off-script" whenever you can, will you be able to get something other than what was decided by the company long before you placed the call.

Stick to your plan. Sometimes, in the middle of a negotiation, you realize that you might be able to get more than you've written into your plan. But don't get carried away by your own acting job. Unless there is a clear change of status, don't rewrite your plan on the fly. Don't demand anything beyond what you've already calculated that you rightly deserve. Don't start piling on the "damages." It's easy to make a mistake and say something that will disqualify you.

PREPARATION AND EXECUTION

When you're convinced that you're in the right frame of mind and that you can keep your cool, you're *almost* ready to dial the number. However, just as with any business call, you want to make sure that for as long as it takes, you will not be disturbed or distracted. Here's what this means:

- Pick a quiet time and a quiet place, where you won't be interrupted by spouse, kids, or roommate. Turn off the TV, radio, or stereo.
- Ignore or disable call waiting. If it's important, the caller will leave a message or call back later.
- Have a glass of water nearby.
- Make sure that you have your plan, a pen, and blank paper to take notes.

Prepared, and in the right state of mind, you can dial the number. Be ready to navigate the voice mail maze, to be on hold for a while, and to be shifted around a bit. When that live person finally answers the line, do not immediately jump into your story.

The typical Unscrewed telephone call has three parts:

1. Get the information.
2. Tell your story.
3. Ask for satisfaction (The Unscrewed Promise).

If you've ever been in retail or other kinds of sales, you recognize this as similar to the classic three-step closing technique taught to rookie salespeople since the first Fuller Brush representative knocked on the first kitchen door. Let's go through the steps, one at a time.

Get the Information

Whenever you call a company—for the first, second, or tenth time—you must, without fail, first get as much information as you can about the person you are speaking to.

"XYZ Tech Support. How can I help you?"

Before answering that question, before you've told him why you're calling, *you* need to collect some very important information from *him*. It needs to be the first thing you do. You might not be able to do it later! Once you've revealed that you may be a "problem" customer, he will be much more reluctant to reveal any information.

The information you're looking for goes far beyond just getting his name. You want to gather as much information as you can. You might not get it all, or even most of it—but the more information you can get, the better chance you will have of prevailing if things don't go smoothly. Here's what you want:

- Full name.
- Agent or representative number.
- Call-back phone number. This is not necessarily the number you just called. You don't want to have to hang on hold for another half hour. What you want is the "inside" line, or the "direct" line. It likely won't be toll-free, but you'll save more in time than it will cost you in phone charges.
- Physical location (city, office, and department), official title, and supervisor's name.
- Number of years with the company.
- Does he like his job?
- What does he think of the company?
- Does he get a lot of calls?

I know you may be thinking, *Why all the personal information? I thought this wasn't about getting personal. Everything is supposed to be about business.*

Getting personal information from the representative does not mean that you are going to be making personal comments. You're gathering information that may be useful later. You never know when you will learn something helpful. Customer service representatives are people, too, with lives. By coincidence, if you grew up in the same town or attended the same school, he may be much more inclined to help you.

It may seem unlikely that customer service representatives would reveal all this to you, but you'd be amazed how often they will. I once had a representative answer the job satisfaction question with, "Are you kidding? These guys are assholes. I'm outta here as soon as I can find another job." It was actually a great bit of information to know. It told me that his company loyalty was low, and that he might be more inclined to stretch the rules on behalf of a maligned customer.

The conversation typically goes something like this:

Me: Hi, my name is Ron Burley. What's yours? [*If you ever have to call back, the first thing you're always asked is, "Who did you speak with?"*]

Representative: Roberto.

Me: Do you have an agent number?

Representative: Yes, 783259.

Me: And which office is that?

Representative: I'm in Tampa.

Me: Nice place. And Roberto, if we get cut off, is there a direct number I can call you back at? [*Once again, this should not be the toll-free number. Get an "inside" line.*]

Representative: Sure, 555-284-2827.

Me: Is there an extension?

Representative: Yes, 7838.

[*It's amazing, once you get them answering questions, how far along you can get before they stop you.*]

Me: And who is your supervisor?

Representative: Nancy Booker.

Me: She's in charge of the office?

Representative: No, that's Dan Clarke.

Me: And his title?

Representative: Vice president of Customer Support.

Me: Roberto, that's great. You're really an excellent representative of XYZ Corporation. Sounds as though you've been with the company a while.

Representative: Almost five years.

[*I'm writing it all down. I recommend longhand, so that he doesn't hear the tap of the computer keyboard. This could make him a little wary.*]

Me: You must like it.

Representative: It's okay.

Me: What do you really want to do?

Representative: I want to be an actor, but, you know…

Me: Yeah, tough to get started. Good luck with that. Sounds as though you're pretty busy.

Representative: Has been today, but things are slowing down.

Me: Good, then maybe you'll have time to help me straighten something out.

Notice that I've been on the phone with this guy for several minutes, and I've yet to get to why I'm calling. As pissed off and frustrated as you may be, getting this information is the foundation to getting what you deserve. *Do not shortcut this step.* Get as much information as you can; at the very least, get the representative's name, representative number, call-back phone number, and physical location. Settle for nothing less.

Once you've collected the information, you can put it to immediate good use. Call the representative by his first name, often. This reminds him that he is no longer anonymous. If you've ever been hung up on by a customer service representative, you realize how valuable this can be. I've never had a customer service representative hang up on me when I've done this part right.

Tell Your Story

State your problem concisely, from time of purchase to time of failure. Stick to the facts; how you feel—how you've been hurt or embarrassed—is not pertinent. This is an impersonal business discussion. You don't have to tell the customer service representative that you are pissed off: he already knows. If you act that way, he has well-rehearsed methods for dealing with it. On the other hand, he's probably not prepared to deal with the quiet, tenacious consumer.

HAWAII NO-GO BOY

Just how important getting information from the customer service representative can be is illustrated by a recent interaction I had with a major airline. After years of collecting frequent-flyer miles on my credit card, I'd made flight reservations for a family vacation to Hawaii. A month later, I routinely checked the itinerary online. It was blank. My stomach sank into my socks. I called the airline and was told that I had failed to "apply the miles to the reservation, and therefore the reservation has been canceled. And sorry, but no more seats are available on that flight."

"But I have a confirmation code: A67801."

"Online confirmation codes do not verify transfer of points," she said politely.

"I didn't get it online," I told her. Armed with my notes from a previous call, I challenged her assertion. "Ms. Parker, on June 24 at 7:30 p.m., I spoke with Paunani, agent number 2459. She told me the points had been applied and that we were confirmed on the flight. She gave me the confirmation code. We had a nice conversation; in fact, she told me that she had grown up on Kauai and that her eleven-year-old daughter placed third in the hula competition last summer." Presented with undeniable evidence that I had actually spoken with "Agent 2459," Ms. Parker asked me to hold. Feeling the breeze beginning to blow in my direction, I threw caution to the wind and allowed her to disappear into a fog of Hawaiian slack key guitar. When she returned to the line a minute later, she apologized for the error and, amazingly, found seats for my family. In this case, no information would have meant…no vacation.

Me: Roberto, I'm really glad I've got you on the other end of the line. You see, I'm a good customer of XYZ, but I'm having a bit of a problem. [*Say this even if this is the first time you've ever used the company's product. You're a good customer, right?*]

Representative: I'm sorry to hear that, Mr. Burley.

Me: Thanks for saying that, Roberto. You see, I visited your web site on Wednesday. I read about your photo-editing software. The description said that it worked with the Microsoft Windows operating system. I purchased the software online for $395, using my Visa card. I downloaded the software and installed it. I received the registration codes via e-mail and registered the software online. I was attempting to perform a color adjustment function this afternoon, but I found that the menu for that function was disabled. I consulted the help file and was surprised to learn that the color adjustment function and several others were not available when running the

---

FOR TRAINING PURPOSES ONLY

Record every call you make to Customer Service. "It's illegal," you say. Not if you handle it right. Taping phone conversations is perfectly legal in all U.S. jurisdictions, just as long as both parties to the conversation are aware that the recording is taking place. (In other locations, you may want to consult an attorney before taping.) That's why you often hear the message while waiting on hold for Customer Service, "This call may be recorded for training purposes."

"But they'd never agree to let me record them," you say.

Of course they wouldn't, if you said, "I'm going to record you, just to make sure that you don't try to screw me."

You need to be tactful, clever, and resourceful.

Here's my standard approach, in the middle of getting the rest of the information.

Me: So you're in the Atlanta office?

Representative: Yes.

Me: And your return phone number?

Representative: 555-123-4567, extension 5555.

Me: Boy, I sound just like you guys. [*Chuckle. Then state clearly.*] This call may be recorded for training purposes. [*Little laugh.*] Maybe you could put in a good word for me?

Representative: [*Laughs*] Sure.

Me: [*Laugh*] Thanks. Anyway, here's what's going on with me today, Roberto…

Notice that I told him outright, in plain language, that I was recording the call. He's been informed, and therefore I am within my rights to record the conversation. It is not my problem that the customer service representative might not have taken my statement seriously. I'm just using the company's same twisted prose, to my advantage. Does anyone really believe they record our conversations for "training" purposes? For "their lawyers" is more like it—in case something goes bad with a "problem" customer. I record the conversation for a similar reason, in case something goes bad with a problem business.

The mechanics of recording a call are very easy these days. You don't even need a cassette deck: your personal computer makes a great recording device and is easy to set up. Almost any electronics store has a gadget that will let you get the audio off the phone line and into the input jack on a computer's audio card. You can then use any recording software to save the call to your computer's hard drive. If your computer didn't come with recording software, you can find several free programs by entering "recording software freeware" into any Internet search engine.

software in Microsoft Windows—that they were available only when running a Mac OS.

Ask for Satisfaction

Me: Roberto, these are important functions to me, and therefore, your software falls short of what I need, or expected. I'm sure you can see my point, Roberto. Therefore, I'd like a full refund [*your predetermined acceptable goal*].

[*At this point, say nothing more. It is a time-tested rule of negotiation that once you have stated what you want, he who speaks first, loses.*]

Representative: I'm sorry, but I can't do that, Mr. Burley.

Me: Why is that, Roberto?

Representative: Mr. Burley, it's not our policy to give refunds on downloaded software.

[*There are those incendiary words: "It's not our policy."*]

Me: That's not acceptable, Roberto. May I speak to your supervisor?

Representative: Certainly.

[*I will move as many steps up the Customer Service food chain as I can until I am either satisfied or stumped. Once I get an absolute "We can't do that" from the highest available customer service representative, round one is over.*]

Me: I need to think about this. Thanks for your assistance. I'll call back later.

Now, you can get to work on your Unscrewed Plan for dealing with Roberto and his cohorts. If you are experienced, and confident that you have a successful strategy, you may decide to launch into your plan immediately. But if not, end the call, if just to give yourself a chance to make sure that you know who, and what, you're dealing with.

Although I want to get a certain amount of information from the customer service representative, I want to give as little information of my own as possible. Information is power, and anything you say can be used against you. In 2001, while disputing several long-distance charges on a telephone bill, I happened to mention my two children. The representative said, "Mr. Burley, our records show that someone made those calls: perhaps it was one of your children. We cannot be liable for misbehaving offspring." She was smug. By telling her about my kids, I had given her a viable, though unprovable, reason to deny my claim. Luckily, I was able to counter the attempt: "That number is for the phone line in my home office. It is in a separate building. My children do not have access to it." I chided myself. I had given her too much information. From that point on, when Unscrewing a situation, I have made sure to give as little personal information as possible—usually just my name, address, and account number.

The next story demonstrates how another slip of the tongue turned a good plan into wastepaper.

UNSCREWED TRUE STORY
The Unfriendly Skies

Several years ago, my wife and I were finally able to step out of our busy lives to take a romantic vacation. We'd lived in Hawaii, so we thought Jamaica might be an interesting and enjoyable destination. The only problem with Jamaica is that it is about as far away from our home in the Pacific Northwest as you can go without actually crossing the Atlantic Ocean. It would take four flights to get us to our destination, near the small town of Negril.

We had booked through a travel agent, and I was reviewing the itinerary when I noticed a potential problem. Our first flight, on a small commuter airline, took us to San Francisco, at which point we changed airlines for a first-class cross-continent flight to Miami on one of the major airlines. According to the schedule, the turnaround time at San Francisco International Airport was only forty-five minutes. The change of airlines meant that we would have to find our way from the far northern concourse, D, to the southernmost concourse, A—a distance of about a half mile. Adding to my concern was the knowledge that flights are often delayed going into SFO because of bad weather, primarily its famous fog.

Given the possibility of a foul-weather delay and the cross-airport transfer of bodies and luggage, I decided to see about getting an earlier flight into San Francisco. Five minutes online confirmed that we were on the first flight out. The airline's own arrival chart also showed that the flight was late at the gate more than 50 percent of the time. And if we missed the connection, the rules were that the commuter line would be on the hook for finding us replacement first-class passage. Of course, we'd miss all of our connecting flights later on. It would be a mess.

The only alternative was to fly to the Bay Area the night before, which would give us plenty of time to have a leisurely breakfast, take a taxi to the airport, and check in for our first-class seats to Miami.

There was also a huge upside for the airline. If, in fact, the commuter flight did cause us to miss the connections, the airline would be on the hook for first-class tickets all the way to Kingston, Jamiaca. It was a clear win-win for all involved, so I didn't anticipate any problems in getting the reservation changed.

I checked with the first airline's Internet reservation site and found a flight that arrived just after six on the evening prior to our current reservation. The online site would not let me change the existing reservation, so I located the commuter airline's customer service number on the itinerary and gave them a call.

After climbing out on two limbs of the voice mail tree, I finally reached Kevin, a San Francisco–based customer service representative for the commuter line.

"Hi, my name is Ron Burley. My wife and I are booked on your flight 123 on July 16."

"Can you wait one moment please as I locate your record?" Kevin spoke crisply and with a vocal flair that seemed to me to identify him as a member of San Francisco's large gay population.

"Here it is," he said. "Yes. Ron and Hali Burley, departing Eugene at 6:05 a.m. and arriving in SFO at 7:35 a.m. Is there a problem?"

"Not really," I said. I explained the situation with the connecting flight, the distance between the gates, and what I'd learned about the on-time record of the commuter flight. "So I had an idea. You've got a flight the night before, with plenty of seats still available. We'd like to change our tickets to that flight so that we don't put your company in the position of having to pay for a couple of first-class tickets to Miami if you fail to deliver us in time to make our connection."

"No problem," said Kevin. "There will be a change fee of $100 per ticket. Would you like to put that on a credit card?"

"I don't think you understand," I said. "I'm trying to save your airline the cost of a pair of first-class tickets from San Francisco to Miami. I'm not even asking that you pay for the hotel. We'll take care of that. You've got the space. We want a relaxed vacation, and we don't want to worry about whether we're going to have trouble making our flight connections."

"I understand what you are saying, Mr. Burley," Kevin said, a little tersely, as if I'd asked something unreasonable. "However, the ticket you hold is nontransferable without paying the $100 per ticket change fee."

"Do you think it's fair to charge us the change fee even if I'm trying to save your airline a lot of money, and save my wife and me a lot of hassle?" I asked plaintively. "It's a win-win situation. Why should we be penalized for trying to help you save a few thousand dollars in replacement tickets, which is a likely event if your flight into San Francisco is true to its record?"

"There's nothing I can do, Mr. Burley. As I said, it's airline policy."

Those words poked at my sternum like a dull butter knife. Nonetheless, I thought I'd try an appeal to his compassionate side. "Kevin, imagine if you were taking this trip with your boyfriend and—"

"You have no right to be making comments about my sexual orientation!" Kevin blasted back. "Who do you think you are? My lifestyle has nothing to do with this conversation, and I am offended that you would presume to think so."

At that moment, I felt like slamming my head against a wall. He was right. In trying to make a simple, unthreatening, politically correct analogy, I'd stepped over the line. I'd made a comment about his sexual identity, or

what I presumed it to be, and had been instantly disqual-
ified from the negotiation.

Nothing could be done.

Once again, there was no technique in my kit bag that I could pull out to Unscrew myself. "I'm sorry, Kevin," I said. "I apologize for offending you. Thank you for your time." I hung up.

Undoubtedly, Kevin would make a note in our reservation file that I was a troublemaker, thereby killing any chance I might have of negotiating this particular situation with another representative. After catching a few breaths of fresh air on our porch, regrouping to the rhythmic chants of countless green tree frogs, I once again called the commuter carrier's Customer Service line.

"I need to reschedule a flight on July 16," I said. "And here's the credit card number for the change fee."

ANATOMY OF A PERSONAL VISIT

For most people, the idea of walking up to an adversary and confronting him or her face-to-face is scary. Others have little problem going toe-to-toe with another person. But it's fair to say that most of us generally want to avoid conflict. Normally, that's a good trait. In the Unscrewed world, it still is.

The in-person visit is not an opportunity to engage in battle with your adversary. It is your opportunity to impress upon the person who is ripping you off—taking advantage of or ignoring you—that you are earnestly determined to get what you deserve.

Why make an in-person visit, given that the phone call techniques work very well? Because, although all the Unscrewed techniques are very powerful, none of them *guarantees* success. Everything we do is about improving the chances that your opponent will come to see things your way. A personal visit is another way to bend the odds in your favor. And just as you may be averse to conflict, a company owner or manager may feel the same way. He or she might have difficulty explaining to you, in person, why he or she is mistreating you. It's much easier to dismiss you when you are a disembodied voice at the other end of a telephone than when you are standing in the company lobby, demonstrating your insistence on making your point.

This is not a lion attacking a bear in its den. You are not there to embarrass your opponent. It may be fun to imagine that you are a movie character, standing on a crate and shouting to all who will listen, "I'm mad as hell, and I'm not going to take it anymore!" But it won't get you anywhere, except out the door.

A personal visit is a low-key, low-energy presentation—devoid of anger, attitude, or rancor. Just as you do on the telephone, smile and keep the tone light. Your words will carry the full weight of your Unscrewed Promise. You are "Just a Little Bit Jack." You are conducting a business negotiation. Your manner, tone of voice, and presentation must represent your determination to get what you deserve, not a conflict to be resolved. Above all, at no point can you step over the line and be perceived as a physical threat to the person or property. Those kinds of threats are instant disqualifiers and will get you ejected from the premises. Remember, to the exact degree that you fail to act in a businesslike manner, the business decision maker will be able to dismiss your Unscrewed Promise. You won't seem as though you are a potential threat to the company's cash flow. You'll just be another crazy person making baseless threats.

The personal visit is very much an acting job, because even though you are acting calm and businesslike, inside, you are likely fuming. You might want to reach across the counter and grab the smug jerk by the collar and shake some sense into him—once again, not a recommended technique.

The anatomy of a personal visit is similar in some ways to a phone call, but different in others. As with a phone call, during your research you will have identified the decision maker whom you need to speak with. Unlike a phone call, there is no chance for the decision maker to put you on hold or hang up on you. You will be there, and the decision maker will have to deal with you. For this reason, if possible, I prefer the in-person visit. I usually take less than an hour out and back, and that includes a stop for a no-whip latté.

PREPARATION AND EXECUTION

Once again, we are assuming that you have made the "give them a chance to do the right thing" phone call to the company, asked for an appropriate resolution, and been rejected.

The main difference between the telephone call and the personal visit is that by the time you are in the store or office, you are prepared to "go all the way." You have decided on your technique and will be ready to implement it as soon as you are rejected the second time.

Preparation for an in-person visit means setting the stage, getting in costume, and making sure that you have all your props ready.

Your stage will be your opponent's turf. You want to decide whether it's best to show up when there are a lot of people around, or when the place is quiet. This may depend upon the technique you use. In either case, you may have to do some research to find out the best time of day. I often make a call simply to ask my opponent when the slow time is. You can also ask what times to avoid—the busy times. (That's the time to be passing out $20 bills.)

Your costume will depend on the type of business. You will want to be the best-dressed person in the room. That does not mean wearing a tux to a tire store. In that case, I'd wear pressed slacks with a belt, hard shoes, and an open-collared shirt. Women should aim for a similar feel, if not the same look. On the other hand, if you're dealing with a bank, you will want to be in a suit. At all times, remember that you are stepping forward as a business equal, negotiating a financial arrangement. The more your opponent is convinced that you are credible—in what you ask for and what you promise to do—the more likely it is that you will get what you deserve.

The props for an in-person visit can be simple or elaborate. You want to have something, though. Just making the promise to pass out flyers in front of a store carries little weight. But if you've got fifty flyers printed, in a folder lying on the desk, your opponent will have little question about your determination to follow through on your promise to do your duty to spread the word to your fellow citizens about how you have been treated. If your opponent doesn't make a decision right away, he or she will know that you have the ability to step outside immediately and start losing the business money. (In the Unscrewed True Story "The Bait-and-Switch Tire Store," it took Mitch about five seconds to do the math and realize the proper business response to the situation.)

Most of your props will be paper flyers, letters, or other information, easily contained in a manila folder. I don't recommend carrying the folder in a briefcase or portfolio. Although it may make you look more businesslike, there's nothing like a bright manila folder to catch the attention of a businessperson. Not many good things come walking in the door dressed in manila.

Depending on the type of business, you may or may not want to make an appointment to see the decision maker. The manager of a retail operation is usually there during business hours, except for lunchtime. Decision makers in service businesses, professional organizations, or larger companies with multiple management levels will certainly require an appointment. If you are unable to get an appointment, just showing up at an acceptable time and occupying a space on the reception room couch is a good approach. Make frequent eye contact with the receptionist and anyone else who walks through the room. If anyone else joins you in the waiting area, feel free to begin sharing your story. An alert receptionist will hear you telling the story and make a phone call; then, the doors will start opening.

Just as with a phone call, once you're convinced that you're in the right frame of mind and that you can keep your cool, you're ready to enter the lair of the beast.

- Make sure that you've given yourself plenty of time to negotiate. You don't want to have to leave to pick up the kids from school right in the middle of your presentation.
- Double-check your appearance: hair combed, teeth brushed, and outfit clean. To reiterate, when you are mak-

---

WORKING WITHOUT A NET

I once grabbed the wrong manila folder as I was running out the door to an appointment with a mortgage broker who had double-charged me and refused a refund. I was able to bluff my way through the presentation, never opening the folder, but giving him vivid descriptions of what I held in my hands. The folder became Pandora's Box: if I were to open it, his misdeeds would be exposed for all the world to see, and we would never be able to lock them up again.

Although that situation worked out in my favor, it's a lot easier just to review a checklist to make sure you've got everything you need before you head out the door.

---

ing an in-person visit, dress in a manner that enhances, rather than detracts from, your credibility.

- Make sure you have all your props.
- Triple-read the text of your flyers and ads to make sure that you have no typos. Word processors can help, but they often miss contextually errant words, such as *to* and *two*.
- Rehearse your Promise. It might be the final thing you say during your in-person visit. You do not want to stumble over it. Say it again and again on the way to the meeting, so that it rolls off your tongue smoothly.

Unlike the phone call, the typical personal visit has only two parts:

1. Tell your story.
2. Ask for satisfaction (The Unscrewed Promise).

Tell Your Story

Even if you have spoken with this person before, you want to start at the beginning. Your story will be a list of facts. Just as with the telephone presentation, you will want to avoid any talk of how you feel—how you've been hurt or embarrassed. That is irrelevant in a business discussion.

"Ms. Hart, I've been a longtime customer of Stratton's Furniture Outlet. If you walk through my living room, it looks as though a Stratton's bomb went off in there. Six weeks ago, I purchased a new sofa hideaway bed. We've used it exclusively as a sofa until this weekend. The first night my teenage niece slept on it, the frame cracked. I called the store earlier this week and was told that there was only a thirty-day warranty on this product."

Notice that you do not place blame on anyone. This is a simple narrative of what happened and why you are standing in front of this woman in the first place. Your calm demeanor will, you hope, set her at ease, and build her confidence in being able to take care of the situation. At this point, she thinks that she is looking across her counter at a sheep. She is unaware that you are a wolf.

Ask for Satisfaction

Once you have laid out your story, and she appears bored, it is time to ask for what you deserve. State it clearly and concisely.

"Ms. Hart, upon closer examination, I noticed that there was a large knot in the wood frame where the crack occurred, implying significant manufacturing error and lack of quality control. The gross negligence in manufacture and your initial refusal to correct the situation have undermined my faith in your company's ability to provide satisfaction in this matter. Therefore, I would like a full refund for the product, including the delivery charge. You can pick up the faulty item at my address by appointment."

At this point, you will launch into whatever technique you have chosen for this particular situation. On average, within five minutes, you will receive satisfaction according to your Unscrewed Goal. That's just the way it works.

The next story starts out with a personal visit that quickly goes down the drain.

UNSCREWED TRUE STORY

The Pee Doctors

The relationship between doctor and patient is sacred in our society. The familiarity and trust in a longtime relationship between physician and patient can mean the early diagnosis of a problem that might go unnoticed by someone less familiar with the patient's history. This relationship is even closer when it comes to children. They often see their pediatrician as a second parent, a demigod who can "make the bad things go away." Accordingly, the loss of that relationship can be unsettling for a child.

I'd known Nancy's family since their first child was born. When I was brought into this story, she was the proud mother of three children, ages two to seven. Like any mother of small children, her days were often scheduled down to the minute. Nancy was a wonderful mom, and great at keeping her harried family on schedule.

Near Halloween a few years ago, her seven-year-old son, Ian, began complaining of stomach cramps and trouble urinating. With two other kids in tow, Nancy took Ian to their pediatrician, Joanne, who had been seeing all of the kids since their first well-baby checkup. Dr. Joanne worked in a clinic that was part of the Patient First Medical corporation, or PFI. The physical examination was inconclusive.

"I'm concerned that his symptoms could be an indication of early-onset diabetes," Dr. Joanne told her friend.

Nancy was horrified. "How can we be sure?"

Dr. Joanne ordered a urine analysis. The boy reluctantly peed into the plastic cup, which was sent to a laboratory for testing.

Nancy was told that she should call the office in a few days to get the results, and that they would decide on any additional treatment after that.

Three days later, the dutiful mom called the clinic. The receptionist was apologetic: the original urine sample had been lost, and a new one would be needed.

"But this is really a bad week for us," Nancy said. Her husband was out of town, and she was taking care of the kids all by herself. There was barely a minute free. "I don't know when we can make it back for another appointment."

"Oh, that's not necessary," the receptionist said. "He can just urinate into any clean plastic container with a top, and you can drop it off at the front desk."

"I suppose we could do that," Nancy said, mentally figuring out the modified route she would take to swing by the clinic sometime that afternoon.

Nancy picked her son up from school, and on the way to soccer practice, she had him pee into a red plastic sippy cup. She snapped on the lid. It was just after 3:00 p.m. The clinic was a little out of the way, but with luck, she could make the drop and still be on time for her son's 3:30 p.m. practice.

Her son stayed in the car while Nancy trotted into the clinic. She dashed around a line of three people to get to the counter. She shoved the kiddy cup over the counter to the receptionist and said, "Hi, here's my son's second urine sample. And be sure to tell the technician that if he loses this one, I'll pour the next one over his head."

Several people in line laughed. The receptionist frowned, took the cup, and said, "I'll make sure that he gets it."

Nancy completed the afternoon rounds, made a stop at the grocery store, filled the car with gas, and arrived home just after 6:00 p.m. There was a message light blinking on the answering machine. The message was from the pediatrician. Dr. Joanne's voice was very serious. Nancy braced herself for the news that no mother wants to hear about her child.

"Nancy," said the doctor, "I'm not exactly sure how to tell you this. It's pretty serious."

Nancy's heart plummeted. She sat down abruptly, unsure of how she would handle the news that her child had a serious illness. She'd known other families facing such challenges, but never thought that hers would be one of them. Tears sprang to her eyes. She braced herself for the rest of Joanne's message.

"Did you really threaten one of our staff when you dropped off a urine sample this afternoon? Our receptionist claims that you said you planned to pour urine on one of our lab technicians."

Nancy wasn't sure whether to breathe a sigh of relief or gasp in surprise.

The doctor continued, "Nancy, we have a zero tolerance policy regarding threats against our staff. The receptionist wrote up a report and submitted it to our Grievance Committee. I'm sorry. Call me back as soon as you can."

Nancy couldn't believe what she was hearing. Somehow, in trying to correct the lab technician's mistake, she had become the villain of the story. She tried to reach her friend, but Joanne had already left the office. She did, however, recognize the voice of the receptionist.

"Did you really report me as a threat when I made that joke about the cup of pee?" she asked.

"We have a zero tolerance policy regarding threats," said the receptionist coolly. "I only did what I have been trained to do."

"But I was kidding!"

"That's not the way I heard it."

"Then you're a stupid cow!" Nancy said, and hung up the phone. She tried reaching Joanne at home, but was forced to leave a message.

An hour later, Joanne called back.

"Did you really call our receptionist a cow?"

"Yes, because she is. She knew I was stressed. She knew it was a joke. Half the people in line laughed at it!"

Joanne sighed. "Nancy, your calling her a name over the phone has made things worse. Now, the receptionist is filing a personal grievance, and I've been told that you are not allowed to come to this, or any other, PFI Pediatric Clinic for the next six months. I need to tell you, if the charges are upheld, the ban will become permanent."

Charges? Ban?

"But you've been our doctor since the kids were born!"

"I know, but there's nothing I can do. It's clinic policy and the higher-ups are adamant about protecting the employees. I can give you a referral to another clinic while this is being reviewed."

"My husband and I also go to your clinic. Are we going to have to switch doctors, too?"

"Strangely, no. It's perfectly all right for you to come to your doctor at this clinic. Same for your husband. It's just the children who have been banned."

"But that doesn't make any sense!" Nancy shouted into the phone.

"I know," Dr. Joanne said. "But that's the way it is. PFI has a zero tolerance policy on threats. Each incident is coded to the patient, not to the parent or guardian. I wish I could do something to change this, but it's much bigger than any single doctor."

Something had to be done.

Nancy knew that I'd been working on a book about how consumers could take on businesses and win, so she gave me a call.

"Does it work for doctors, too?" she asked.

"I don't see why not," I replied.

She told me the whole story, including the part where she called the receptionist a cow. I had a few additional questions for her, but she cut me off.

"I've got to take my daughter to ballet," she said. "Do you think you can help me?"

"I'll do my best," I assured her.

A few minutes on the Internet told me most of what I needed to know. The clinic was part of a larger medical corporation, Patient First Medical, Inc. After a little more digging, I was able to locate the phone and fax numbers of the executive offices on a Securities and Exchange Commission document in their "For Investors" section of the company web site.

After ten minutes of writing at my computer, I printed out a single sheet of paper and faxed it to the Office of the President of Patient First Medical, Inc., Dr. Howard Bastman.

Then I called the executive offices and introduced myself.

"PFI. How can I help you?" asked the young woman at the other end of the line.

"Are you near the fax machine?" I asked.

Silence.

"I just faxed a press release to your office. I recommend that you retrieve it from the fax machine and take it immediately to Dr. Bastman."

"One minute please." She put me on hold. As she was not a customer service representative, this did not alarm me. She returned a minute later.

"Hello," she said. "Are you still there?"

"I'm still here. Did you find the press release?"

"Yes. And I gave it to Dr. Bastman. He asked where he could call you in a few minutes."

"I'm on the line right now."

"It will be just a few minutes."

I gave her my number. I supposed the good doctor was checking with his in-house legal staff before getting on the phone with me.

Five minutes later, my phone rang. "Can you please hold for Dr. Bastman?"

"Of course." I've always been puzzled by people who hire other people just to push the buttons on a telephone for them.

Dr. Bastman came on the line. "Mr. Burley, I've read the press release that you sent me, and I'm still not clear what you are asking of us. I must also advise you that because you are not a family member, I cannot release medical records to you."

The man's ego barely fit inside his two titles, doctor and president.

"Dr. Bastman, I won't be needing any medical information. In fact, I'm just offering you an opportunity to respond before I send out my media release."

"You aren't serious?"

"Actually, I am," I replied. "I spent sixteen years in the broadcast business. I think this will make a fantastic story. The television, radio, and newspaper folks will jump all over it. Imagine the visuals: a beautiful, hard-working mother of three, cuddling her three cute children. She's just trying to get through each day with an ounce of sanity left when she makes a joke to a clinic receptionist about pouring pee on the head of a person whom she's never met. Everyone knew that it was a joke, but chose not to act accordingly. It was blown completely out of proportion, to the point where her kids will be cut off from the only doctor who has taken care of them their entire lives. And, in the most ironic twist, the mother still gets to go to the clinic, so the only people being hurt in this exchange are three innocent children."

"I don't quite see it that way," Bastman replied. "We have rules."

"I understand, and you also have choices," I said. "The choice here is whether you can find a way out of a situation that has clearly been blown out of proportion, or whether tomorrow morning you want to find yourself on the front page of the City section of the newspaper in an article titled, 'Pee Doctors Punish Innocent Children.'"

Silence. More silence.

"You're right," he said, finally. "This has been blown out of proportion. Let me see what I can do."

An hour later, a half hour after the close of business, Dr. Bastman called me back.

"Mr. Burley, do you think Nancy would be willing to apologize to the receptionist for calling her what she called her?"

"I'm sure she would. She knew that she was disrespectful."

"In that case," Bastman continued, "we're willing to over-look the first incident. It was clearly a joke. Not a very good one, but certainly not a threat. Is that acceptable?"

"I believe it will be perfectly acceptable, Doctor. Nice doing business with you."

I don't think he felt quite the same way. "Good night, then," were his parting words.

Nancy's kids were reinstated as clients of the PFI Pediatric Clinic the following morning. It sure would have been fun to send out the "Pee Doctors" press release; the folks at PFI deserved some grief for what they'd put Nancy through. But that would have been revenge—never part of a good Unscrewed Plan.

FIVE TECHNIQUES FOR DEALING WITH SMALL BUSINESSES

Relationships with small businesses can be among the most rewarding in the world of commerce. Conversely, small-business operators can be among the most obstinate and unprofessional people you'll ever encounter on the other side of a cash drawer. They are often enthusiastic about what they do, and just as often have poor business judgment. Many of them have little business training or education. They may be nice people doing what they think is right, but be terrible businesspeople, undermining their own success with arbitrary or absurd policies and practices.

HER OWN WORST ENEMY

A friend of mine runs a silk clothing boutique in San Francisco. Early on, she had a store policy that trying on clothing was not allowed: skin oils would soil the silk fabric. For the same reason, she didn't allow merchandise returns, even for store credit. Needless to say, she was having a rough go of it. She'd received countless complaints about the policies during the two years she'd been in business, but wouldn't budge. With her business failing, she came to me for help.

After several consulting sessions where she huffed and spit and swore, I finally convinced her to change her ways. Thereafter, she kept a set of "try on for size" items, which she laundered regularly. I also convinced her to take returns for store credit; she would then launder the returns and sell them at cost. Those two changes turned her business around. She's a very nice woman. She was trying hard to stay in business, but couldn't see that the problem was with her policies and not unreasonable customers.

I still think, though, of the hundreds of unsatisfied customers she pissed off and turned away during her first two years in business. They are gone, along with all the word-of-mouth referrals they could have generated.

FRIENDS AND NEIGHBORS

Small businesspeople are often members of your community, unlike the faceless, disembodied voices on the corporate Customer Service line. Their kids are on your kid's soccer team. You run into them at the grocery store, restaurant, or movie theater. You attend the same PTA meetings, sports events, or religious organization.

It is exactly this day-to-day interaction that can take a Customer Service call from formally polite to fractiously personal very quickly. As adults, we haven't progressed much from high school. Many people still care a great deal what their friends and neighbors think of them. That can work for us—or against us.

When Unscrewing a locally owned or locally managed small business, we must take extra care to be businesslike and not make the conversation a personal attack. We also want to make very clear that we want only what is fair, and that the alternative will involve a very public display of our dissatisfaction.

DON'T JUMP THE GUN

We want our small businessperson to make the smart business decision, even if he or she doesn't have a lot of business smarts. We want to give the individual a way to keep some dignity, even if he or she was planning on keeping your money. When dealing with a small businessperson, this implies that at the time of your negotiation, no one else has been told of the disagreement.

If you have already sent a flame-mail to all your Internet buddies, or trashed the guy's reputation at the Rotary Club, he'll likely feel that the damage has already been done. He may feel that he was blindsided by your actions, even though you gave him at least two chances. So why should he give you a nickel?

Therefore, do not say a word to anyone about your disagreement, or your impending negotiation, until you have delivered your Promise, initiated your Plan, and received a response.

WHAT WE KNOW VERSUS WHAT WE SAY

In each of the techniques, there is often a big difference between what we say to our adversary and our true desires or intentions. I don't *really* want to stand on sidewalks or take out newspaper ads. However, each technique is really an extension of the Promise. Your adversary must be absolutely convinced that you are willing to spend an unlimited amount of time, effort, and energy to get what you deserve. Think of Clint Eastwood in *Dirty Harry* when he says, "Did I use six bullets or seven? I don't remember. Do you feel lucky?" You are counting on your adversary to understand what's at stake and to make the wise business decision—before you ever have to print, fax, e-mail, or picket.

There's a little bit of the actor in all of us. Each technique is a scene, where you are the actor on a stage, with props to help you tell your story.

OUR CIVIC DUTY

I'll remind you again: you must never directly threaten an individual, a company, or even a company's cash flow. People might become very angry. Attorneys could get involved. The situation could get very messy and expensive.

In the implementation of any Unscrewed technique, you are performing your civic duty, using your constitutionally guaranteed right of free speech, to spread an alert to your fellow citizens. The exact wording is not as important as understanding the intent and goal of each technique.

SMALL-BUSINESS TECHNIQUE NUMBER ONE: THE TOWN CRIER

Type: In-person visit.

Upside: Inexpensive, quick results.

Downside: Time-intensive (one to eight hours, if implemented).

Props & Tools: One manila folder, fifty copies of "My Horror Story with [business name]" flyer.

Optional: "I Got Screwed by [business name]" picket sign.

In old England—before the era of daily newspapers and twenty-four-hour satellite networks—folks would get their news from the town crier. This fellow would stand on a box in the middle of the village square and read the news of the day, mostly pronouncements from the reigning sovereign, with a little gossip thrown in.

The Unscrewed version of the town crier involves taking advantage of your free speech rights on the piece of sidewalk closest to your adversary's front door. This is the technique that I used in the Unscrewed True Story "The Unscrupulous Car Dealer."

The Unscrewed Promise for "The Town Crier"

"Mr. Acorn, you've been in business in this town for many years, and therefore I was hoping that you would find a way to do the right thing and [*your acceptable goal*]. It hasn't turned out that way.

"I consider it my civic duty to inform my fellow citizens of exactly how I've been treated by your company. In this folder, I have 100 flyers that tell my story. By tomorrow morning, I'll also have a nice-looking sign urging people not to shop at your store. Spending my weekends on the sidewalk in front of your store may not get me a dollar of what you owe me, but I'll feel a lot better knowing that I've done the right thing and saved countless people the trouble I've had dealing with you. "

After this, the one who speaks first, loses.

Let's take a look at this technique, sentence by sentence and paragraph by paragraph.

Paragraph 1: "Mr. Acorn,...turned out that way."

You are reminding him of his position in the community, expressing your regret for what you are about to do, and restating your acceptable goal. It is important not to appear gleeful, or even smirk. I guarantee that it would be read the wrong way.

Paragraph 2, Sentence 1: "I consider it my civic duty... treated by your company."

This is the opening line of your Promise. You are stating your motivation: civic duty, rather than revenge. Revenge implies a battle. Moral zealotry implies a crusade. No small businessperson, manager, or employee wants to become the target of a crusade. (Pity the poor bus driver who ejected Rosa Parks from that bus. It started a 381-day boycott of the transit service, elevated Dr. Martin Luther King Jr. to national prominence, and crushed a century of segregation in the South. And you know what? He was just "following company policy.")

Paragraph 2, Sentences 2 and 3: "In this folder,...not to shop at your store."

The folder should be a standard, unlabeled manila office folder. You may never have to open it. One woman succeeded in getting her way with a car dealer just by being armed with the knowledge that she had an ace in the hole: fifty flyers. The flyers should include a simple headline that reads something like, "Acorn Company Mistreats Its Customers." The body of the flyer should be your story, in simple, noninflammatory terms. Close with, "I'm asking for what I deserve." At the bottom, add your phone number or e-mail address. You can print the flyers on colored paper—not too dark, though: the print should be easily readable. If you don't want to give out your phone number or e-mail address, that's fine. You can get a temporary e-mail address at one of the major Internet portals, such as Yahoo! or Google, so that you don't need to use your personal e-mail address. This will not only prevent regular spam, should the flyers get into the wrong hands, but it will also prevent the business owner or employees from harassing you, should they choose the low road. (An example flyer is available on the Unscrewed web site: www.unscrewed.biz).

Paragraph 2, Sentence 4: "Spending my weekends...dealing with you."

With this closing line, you are telling your adversary that you are not going away, that you will become a fixture in front of his establishment for an indefinite period of time. He can do the mental equation of how much business he could lose, relative to the cost of taking care of you. As long as the conversation has remained polite, impersonal, and nonconfrontational, he can make a business decision to make things right with you, even if he thinks that it is wrong, against policy, or against his nature. It's just a business decision.

In my experience, the vast majority of businesspeople will make the correct decision at this point if what you are asking for is reasonable. However, if Mr. Acorn is silent for more than thirty seconds, tells you to go away, or otherwise disputes what you have said, *do not say a word.* Exit the store. Stand on the sidewalk and start handing out those flyers. Only once have I had to do this; the proprietor was at my shoulder in less than five minutes, ready to make the correct business decision.

There is always the chance that your adversary is one of the really stupid ones, or someone who takes all challenges personally. According to your assessment, you will know how much time is appropriate to give to your Plan before it becomes unprofitable.

SMALL-BUSINESS TECHNIQUE NUMBER TWO: SUNDAY SUPPLEMENT

Type: In-person visit.
Upside: Minimal time commitment, quick results.
Downside: Expensive ($300–$1000, if implemented).

Props & Tools: One manila folder, one prepared newspaper advertisement, one printout of the local newspaper's rate card.

This is a variation of "Small-Business Technique Number One: Town Crier." Instead of flyers and placards, an advertisement in the local newspaper is used as the potential club. You may recognize this technique from the Unscrewed True Story "The Remodeling Contractor."

The technique works because of the sheer audacity of the notion that you might actually place a newspaper advertisement complaining of how you've been treated. It's a great example of how your real goal may differ from your message. Your goal is simple: to be made whole financially. But the message you're sending your opponent is that money is *not* the object. Your opponent gets the message that you are some kind of consumer crusader and that he or she has somehow become your latest cause. At this point, most businesspeople are more than willing to meet your meager financial request, rather than face the question at the country club, "What did you do that made that fruitcake start taking out newspaper ads lambasting your company?"

It is important not to point out to your opponent the obvious possibility of personal embarrassment or public shame. You stick to your "truth-telling" motivation; your opponent will recognize the personal downside.

The downside for you is that if you actually end up printing the ad, it can be expensive. However, if you're talking about a $60,000 remodeling job gone bad, a few hundred dollars to place a newspaper advertisement is chicken feed. (When your adversary finally makes the correct business decision, be sure to have him or her deduct the cost of the ad from your bill.)

The Unscrewed Promise for "Sunday Supplement"
"Ms. Spencer, I know you are a professional. However, I am so completely disappointed with the services you have provided and your reluctance to [*your acceptable goal*], that I feel compelled to protect my fellow citizens from a similar fate."

[*Open manila folder containing ad and rate card.*]

"This is the ad I'm going to run. You'll notice the bottom line, where I ask for similar stories. I thought that might be helpful in case we want to run a second series. Here is the rate sheet for the local daily. I've decided on a five-by-seven in the Sunday supplement.

"As you can see, it's a little costly, but I think that the good feeling I'll get knowing that hundreds of my fellow citizens will be prevented from suffering a similar fate will make it worth it."

After this, the one who speaks first, loses.

Let's take a look at this technique, sentence by sentence and paragraph by paragraph.

Paragraph 1, Sentences 1 and 2: "Ms. Spencer…from a similar fate."

Once again, you are reminding your opponent of his or her position in the community and what your opponent stands to lose. You are restating your acceptable goal and reasons for taking action: your duty to your fellow citizens.

Paragraph 2: "This is the ad…Sunday supplement."

The more realistic the ad looks, the better. If you have a graphics layout program, such as Adobe Illustrator or Corel Draw, you should create the ad in its real size and print it out with the printer's registration marks. It's an added detail that shows that the ad is real and ready to be sent to the publisher. If not, create a five-by-seven-inch box on a letter-size document, and lay out your ad in there. The ad I created when dealing with the contractor had his company name inside a red circle with a line across it, implying "Don't do business with this guy!" The ad included my name and phone number. It also gave a web site name: www.dontgowithabcconstruction.com. If you want, you can register the web site and get it going for $10 or so. Write your story and put it up on the web. (You can decide whether it fits inside the time and expense allotment of your plan.) On the bottom of the flyer, I added, "More ABC Construction Horror Stories Wanted." Having a copy of the rate sheet from the newspaper reinforces the idea that you are serious. You can usually download or print the rate sheet from the newspaper's web site. Stapling a note with the name of the advertising coordinator on the corner of the price sheet is a nice touch, too.

Paragraph 3: "As you can see...will make it worth it."

A single look at the rate sheet will tell your opponent that you are willing to spend several hundred dollars to make your point. That alone slips you across the line into the "little bit crazy" category. The mention of running a second series takes you over the top. You must deliver these lines in a matter-of-fact, unthreatening tone. You are stating one component of a business transaction, not making threats. Leave it up to the businessperson's own imagination what the downside to his or her business and reputation will be. Once again: no smiles, sneers, or grins. Your opponent needs to believe that your action is as inevitable as the onset of winter if he or she fails to take care of you.

The very public nature of this technique, if actually applied, can rock the foundations of a small town or city. The conflict between you and your adversary will become very public. Do not be surprised if you get calls from the local media. If you're not prepared for that, then it's in your best interests to do your most brilliant sales job up front: convincing your adversary in a quiet, determined "Clint Eastwood" voice that you are absolutely intent on placing the ad and that you are so obsessed with getting what you are due that you will let it run for an indefinite period of time, collect "me too" stories, and share those stories in media interviews.

Given the high-profile nature of implementing this technique, you may consider adding one line, something like, "I don't want this to turn into a public debate, but I will do so, unless we can come to terms on this right here, right now."

Be careful. Don't let your real anger show through. Be sure to stay businesslike, calm, and impersonal.

SMALL-BUSINESS TECHNIQUE NUMBER THREE: BUY-BYE CUSTOMERS

Type: In-person visit.
Upside: Minimal time commitment, quick results.
Downside: Moderately expensive ($240, if implemented).
Props & Tools: One manila folder, a dozen copies of competitor's Yellow Pages ad, a dozen $20 bills.

This Unscrewed technique is my favorite, because it is the most audacious of the in-person visits. "Buy-Bye Customers" is a raise-the-stakes game of how many customers you can pay to go somewhere else before your opponent decides to take care of you. This is the technique I used in the Unscrewed True Story "The Bait-and-Switch Tire Store."

The Unscrewed Promise for "Buy-Bye Customers"

"Jake, it looks as though the shop's having a busy day—lots of customers waiting in line just to pay you money. I am so appalled with the way you have treated me, and your refusal to [*your acceptable goal*], that I feel I have a solemn obligation to use my First Amendment right of free speech to tell each of them how poorly I've been treated by your company.

"It's not about the money. I'm even willing to invest some extra cash of my own to help them save themselves."

[*Open the plain, unlabeled manila folder containing copies of Yellow Pages ad and $20 bills.*]

"Right here, I have a dozen copies of your competitor's Yellow Pages ad, with the address circled, and a $20 bill stapled to the corner. I am going to tell my story to as many of those people standing in line as I can, handing them the Yellow Pages ad and a $20 bill if they agree just to try the guy across the street. Then, I'll stand on the sidewalk in front of your store and warn customers before they even make it to your door.

"Yes, I know it'll cost me a few bucks, but I'll sure feel good about saving them from going through what I've gone through doing business with you."

After this, the one who speaks first, loses.

Let's take a look at this technique, sentence by sentence and paragraph by paragraph.

Paragraph 1: "Jake, it looks as though…treated by your company."

Pointing out that he's having a busy day puts the potential loss right on the table. If he is having a slow day, you could point out how he'd hate to lose the few customers he has. You are also reminding him of your dissatisfaction, restating your acceptable goal, and informing him of your determination to protect your fellow citizens from his poor business practices.

Paragraphs 2 to 4: "You see, Jake,…to your door."

To many business owners, this is about the most absurd thing they've ever heard. You've been after them to compensate you a certain amount, yet here you are, willing to sacrifice even more, because "it's not about the money." It is an entirely illogical position, but there you are with $20 bills stapled to Yellow Pages ads.

Paragraph 5: "Yes, I know…doing business with you."

Telling your adversary that you'll feel better saving some souls clearly puts you in the category of "crazy zealot." He'll quickly do the math and figure out that it will be much cheaper to take care of you than to let you start telling your story and paying people to go away. If each customer is planning on spending the same amount that you did, his downside is twelve times whatever your total bill was.

This technique is an excellent example of why you don't first yell, "Fire!" and then ask for a fire extinguisher. Conventional wisdom would be to stand in the lobby and start shouting about how badly you've been treated. Some customers might believe you and go away. However, once they've gone away, you've lost your negotiating advantage, because your financial leverage is the possibility that he will lose business. If it's already gone, you've got nothing to negotiate with, and he's got no reason to change his mind in your favor.

The dialogue must be matter-of-fact. Make no threats or slanderous statements. Once again, you are a citizen of the community, dedicated to protecting your brothers and sisters from the evils of malevolent business owners.

SMALL-BUSINESS TECHNIQUE NUMBER FOUR: SPOKESPERSON FOR THE COMPETITION

Type: Telephone, fax.

Upside: Minimal time commitment.

Downside: Response time may be slow (a day or so, compared with a few minutes for the previous in-person techniques).

Props & Tools: Telephone and fax machine. Fax letter telling how you've been mistreated by [*business name*]. Fax cover sheet providing permission to reproduce and quote the letter.

Standard business logic is that, if a company is in a very competitive industry, it will struggle to keep every customer. However, as we've discussed in earlier chapters, some companies elect to eject customers they feel may cost them more than they are worth. Even small companies do this. Usually, they figure you are going to take more time than you are worth. Other times, the inefficiency is their fault. A building contractor may have underbid your contract and then may try to get out of it or do the job with inexpensive labor or lower-quality materials than promised.

"Spokesperson for the Competition" works very well with small companies that have strong local competition. I've used this technique successfully with a lawn care service, a car dealer, and a mortgage broker. It is the most succinct of all the Unscrewed techniques.

The Unscrewed Promise for "Spokesperson for the Competition"

"Ms. Kennedy, I understand that you are in a very competitive business, which is why I fail to understand why you would treat me the way you have. It would have been much simpler to come to terms with me by just [*your acceptable goal*]. Accordingly, I feel compelled to do what I can to protect my fellow customers.

"I am about to fax you a letter that, tomorrow at 3 p.m., I will also be faxing to each of your competitors, including [*her number one competitor if you know it*]. I will also send them a letter granting permission to use my name, share the letter, and provide my phone number to any customer who might be considering doing business with your company."

After this, the one who speaks first, loses.

Let's take a look at this technique, sentence by sentence and paragraph by paragraph.

Paragraph 1: "Ms. Kennedy, I understand…fellow customers."

You are letting her know that you are aware of the competitive nature of her business. You restate your acceptable goal and then establish your motivation for taking action: civic duty, rather than revenge.

Paragraph 2: "I am about to fax…with your company."

You concisely state what you are about to do, leaving all the suppositions about how your "free speech" actions will affect the bottom line up to her. You make it clear that this will be a tool that the competition can use freely in the competitively charged atmosphere of her industry.

The key to this technique is the content of the letter. It must be absolutely factual, without hyperbole or other embellishment. It should be written in plain "consumer speak" rather than business language. If you have beautiful and legible handwriting, you can pen it yourself. Otherwise, a nicely printed letter in a standard serif font (Times New Roman, for example) will work best. (Sans serif fonts, such as Helvetica and Arial, look too slick and commercial.) Keep it short—maybe only a couple of paragraphs.

The opening of the letter should read something like this:

"Dear Fellow Consumer:

I am writing to alert you to a terrible experience I had with [*business name*]."

Tell your story briefly, though in vivid language (no foul language).

You can write about the following:

- "repeated attempts to work things out"
- "their failure to make any attempts to satisfy you"
- "uncaring treatment of a loyal customer"
- "unprofessional behavior"
- "hostile attitude when asked for help"

MULTIPLYING TO THE RIDICULOUS

There is a sales technique called *reducing to the ridiculous.* You've probably been the victim of it. Here's how it goes: "Mr. Burley, I know that $4,000 may seem like a lot of money to pay for a television set. However, its projected life is ten years. That's only $400 per year, or about $1 per day. I know that you and your family will get many hours of enjoyment from this fantastic machine. Isn't that worth $1 a day?"

Our version is called multiplying to the ridiculous. It can be useful when making your case to small-business owners.

"Ms. Schmidt, I know you've said that you're not going to give me a refund because the warranty expired a week ago. This is a $400 item. You might like to know that I've spent an average of $500 per year in your store for the past five years. Not your biggest customer, but if I keep that up, that will be $2,500 worth of business coming your way in the next five years. My best friend is also a regular customer. Let's say she spends the same amount, but stops doing business with you because of how you've treated me. If we each share my story with only two of our other friends and they decide to take their business elsewhere, that would be an additional $5,000 in lost business. So let me get this straight: you are willing to sacrifice $10,000 in future business over the return of a $400 item that is a week out of warranty. Does that make sense?"

You should "highly recommend that no one do business with them."

You will also need to declare that "I have no connection, financial or otherwise, with any other company. I am only writing to warn other potential customers, so that they won't go through the difficulties that I went through."

The strongest letter will include your request for them to call you, though this will require you to include your phone number. However, assuming that this letter will never actually have to be sent to any competitors, I recommend including it at this point; you can take it out later.

Read through the letter several times. Edit out big words and complex sentences in favor of simple, heartfelt language.

The cover letter to your adversary's competitors should be short and straightforward: "I am writing to share this story with you. I am giving you my permission to share it with any of your customers, so that they will not have to go through what I went through." They will know what to do with it from there.

SMALL-BUSINESS TECHNIQUE NUMBER FIVE:
TENACITY IS MY MIDDLE NAME

Type: Telephone, fax, U.S. mail, in-person visit.
Upside: Minimal time commitment.
Downside: Response time may be slow. You may need to follow up with another technique.
Props & Tools: Telephone, fax machine, and your mailbox.

This could also be called "The Squeaky Wheel Gets the Grease." You want your adversary to feel that you are going to badger him every day for the next thousand years. You want him to be in fear that you are going to shower him relentlessly—via phone, fax, U.S. mail, and visits—with:

- obscure quotations from law books,
- not necessarily pertinent decisions by regulatory agencies,
- newspaper and magazine clippings about customer service,
- letters demanding answers to heartfelt questions, and
- competitors' ads.

You also want him to believe that you are going to show up in front of his store, at the busiest times, to "share your story." The perfect attitude for this is "Just a Little Bit Jack."

The Unscrewed Promise for "Tenacity Is My Middle Name"

"As I see it, Bob, you and I have a disagreement here. You don't want to do what's right. I think you should. I know you're a busy man and that I might not seem that important to you. All I've been asking for is [*your acceptable goal*].

"I've been reading a lot, and there are some magazine articles I'm going to fax you that might help you along. I've got some law books, too, and I'm sure there's stuff in there. I'll stop by [*at his busiest time*], and we can look through a few of the volumes.

"Since my operation, I've had far too much time on my hands. My wife's been saying I need a hobby. You know what, Bob? *You* can become my hobby. I can spend my days standing in front of your store, performing a legitimate community service by telling folks just how you've treated me. Hell, I could use one of those little hand clickers to count how many unsuspecting souls I actually save from your regrettably destructive business practices. My doctor told me that fresh air would be good for me. What do you think, Bob? Do you want to become my hobby?"

After this, the one who speaks first, loses.

Let's take a look at this technique, sentence by sentence and paragraph by paragraph.

Paragraph 1: "As I see it, Bob,…all I've been asking for is…"

You are reminding him that he is a busy person—and you are not. You are also restating your acceptable goal.

Paragraph 2: "I've been reading…a few of the volumes."

You are painting a picture of how you are going to bury your adversary with probably irrelevant, possibly meaningless, and definitely annoying factual material.

Paragraph 3: "Since my operation…become my hobby?"

You've just given him a verbal tour of hell on earth. He may consider making a call to his lawyer to see about a restraining order, until he realizes it would only keep you out of his store—not keep you from telling your story—and that it would be less expensive, time-consuming, and troublesome simply to settle with you.

This is the only technique where you are pretty safe running wild with your acting. Keep your voice calm, but you sure can put a joyous smile in it—as if you had just found the calling you had been seeking for many years.

It is very important not to say anything that could even indirectly be interpreted as physically hostile, menacing, or threatening. It is a small step from "Just a Little Bit Jack" to "Just a Little Bit Ted Bundy." Several years ago, one Unscrewed seminar attendee thought he'd successfully implemented this technique, until the police knocked on his door. Apparently, during his conversation with a business owner, he had indirectly mentioned the woman's daughter. She'd agreed to his terms, but immediately called the authorities, claiming he had threatened her child. "Do not pass Go. Do not collect $200." He was able to convince the police that he was not a threat, but he had inadvertently given his adversary the weapon she needed to avoid keeping her part of the bargain.

The next story demonstrates how I convinced a major corporation to give me the product, and the refund, too.

––––––––––––––

UNSCREWED TRUE STORY
The Terrible Travel Agency

Several years ago, I received one of those phone calls that we all dread, news that a beloved family member had died. In this case, it was my maternal grandmother from Reno, who had taken care of me for much of my early life. Just three months previously, I was the one who had told her it was time for her to move into a nursing home. Until that point, the game had been, "How long can I stay in my house?" When she reached ninety-four, we knew the answer.

With a heavy heart, I went to my favorite online travel site, Ventura Travel, to book flights and a hotel for my wife and me. I would fly down first to help make plans for the funeral. Hali would follow in a couple of days to attend the service and burial.

My plane landed three hours late in the middle of a January snowstorm. I retrieved a rental car and slogged my way to the hotel. Valet parking was snowed in. I parked in a distant lot and dragged my roll-along suitcase through the drifts to the hotel reception area. After waiting in line for a half hour behind a couple of plump men wearing purple jackets and bucket hats with gold braid, I was finally face-to-face with Jan, one of four harried front desk clerks.

"Welcome, Mr. Burley, I apologize for the wait," said the blonde twenty-something.

"No problem. I don't have anywhere to be right now." I wasn't going to meet with the rest of the family until morning.

"Ummm," Jan said as she scanned her computer screen. For the well traveled, it was an alarm bell.

"Is anything wrong?" I asked.

"I know we promised you a nonsmoking room," she replied. "But there aren't any left. I'm sorry."

I'm not usually too picky about hotel rooms: just don't give me the one next to the elevator. Hali, on the other hand, is absolutely firm about needing a nonsmoking room. The one time we'd capitulated regarding that requirement, she'd spent the whole night sneezing.

"Are you sure?" I asked, palming a $20 bill in her direction. "My wife really needs a nonsmoking room."

Jan looked at the bill, and then looked me in the eye. "I absolutely would if I could, but we've got a convention going, and every last room is booked and occupied. If you had been here an hour ago, I might have been able to squeeze you in somewhere, but not now."

"We were guaranteed a nonsmoking room," I said, showing her the online reservation.

"I can see that," Jan said. "And I understand your wife's situation, too. I've got the same problem. You're not booked with the convention, so you don't really need to be at this hotel. Let's see whether I can't find you a nonsmoking reservation at another nearby facility. Would that be all right?"

"That would be wonderful."

Five minutes later, Jan was giving me directions to another hotel, about a mile away. Half an hour later, I was snugly asleep in a king-size bed in a nonsmoking room.

The funeral took a lot out of all of us. Grandma had been the anchor of the family. We couldn't help but wonder where the winds would take us without her holding us together.

We arrived home five days after we'd left. It was great to be back, and with our kids. The weight of events hung heavily on me. It took several days for me to catch up on my normal routine, and several days after that before I thought to check with Ventura Customer Service to make sure that I wasn't billed for the first hotel. I was.

"Mr. Burley, you should have called us to make the reservation change," Margie explained. "It's clearly stated in the online contract rules that any changes need to be approved by us prior to making them."

"Margie," I explained, "I was in the middle of a snowstorm without a computer. The desk clerk at the hotel where you booked me actually made the reservation for me. I didn't even do it. Why would I possibly think there was anything wrong with her doing that? *She* didn't tell me. Besides, they were unable to provide the nonsmoking room I had been promised."

"That's our policy, Mr. Burley," Margie said. "It's out of my hands."

"Then, I'm going to have to find out whose hands it *is* in, won't I?"

I can't remember whether it was Margie or me who hung up first.

Something had to be done.

A half hour of searching online revealed nothing in the way of telephone or fax access numbers for the Ventura inner sanctum. Then, I remembered that Ventura had only recently been spun off from its giant parent company. With such a short history as a public company, there would not be much of a trail to follow—online or otherwise. However, as a public company, it would be listed on the stock exchange. That insight sparked an idea about how I might smoke out the person "whose hands it was in."

I logged onto one of the major Internet financial sites, located the Ventura financial page, and entered the online chat room. Financial page chat rooms are rife with rumors, questions, lies, and hype. Despite that, they are places where investors look for tips and trends. A few years ago, a twelve-year-old from Illinois made almost $500,000 by hyping stocks in a chat room. I figured, if you could praise, you could also condemn.

Following is the actual text, with names changed, that I posted in the online chat room.

Anybody who is planning on using Ventura for travel should be aware of a recent experience I had. I was traveling to Reno for a funeral and had booked a non-smoking room at the Ambassador Hotel. My wife is allergic to cigarette smoke. Anyway, when I got there, the hotel said they didn't have a nonsmoking room available. So they actually helped find a nonsmoking room at another hotel. They were great! A week after I got back from the funeral, Ventura said that they would not refund the money I'd paid for the stay at the Ambassador. I told them that the Ambassador actually helped me find the other room, so they clearly knew about it. Ventura didn't care. They said I should have changed the reservation with them. Period. So Caveat Emptor! Ventura Customer Service leaves a lot to be desired. I've been a regular

> customer of theirs for six years. I booked all my company's travel through them. Not anymore! Since going public, they are going downhill. From now on, I'm booking via TravelWorld and recommend that you do, too.
>
> —Ron Burley, Eugene, Oregon

I posted that in the online chat room at 8:10 a.m. Pacific Time, and then fixed some breakfast. Just before 9, I checked to see whether anyone had taken notice. I was shocked to see five new messages, all in the same vein: "Me, too." In the same forty-five-minute period, the Ventura ticker had dropped a half point. Five minutes later, my phone rang.

"Mr. Burley, my name is Veronica Hallstrom. I work for Mr. Eric Goodman, vice president of Customer Relations for Ventura Travel. Would you mind holding for a few seconds while I connect you?"

"No problem," I said, wiping the remnants of a buttered bagel from my fingers.

As promised, Mr. Goodman picked up the line in short order. "Mr. Burley, I've just recently become aware of a problem you brought to the attention of our Customer Service team." His phone smile was wide. "Can you tell me about it?"

I gave him the 10¢ version of the story, as I was certain he'd already read the online entry and any notes from the Customer Service report. "Margie told me it was your policy to make people pay for hotel rooms they never stayed in," I finished.

Mr. Goodman laughed. "That's not exactly how we would put it, though I guess that is the essence of what did happen here."

"Because you clearly were in a special situation and are a valued longtime customer, I would like to do my best to correct this situation."

I wasn't sure where he was going with this. "Me, too."

"Because of all the misunderstandings in this case, we are

going to refund the cost of the hotel stay and the airline flight. Will that be acceptable?"

"Sounds good."

"I hope that you will continue to book your travel with Ventura, and that you will also give us credit for correcting a rare mistake quickly when it was brought to our attention."

"Of course," I said. Finally, I could tell which way the wind was blowing. "Thank you."

"Thank you, Mr. Burley, for bringing this to our attention."

I hadn't been sure where he was coming from, not until his last statement. "Give us credit" could only be a sideways request for me to update my online comment to reflect the stellar customer service I had received from a vice president of the company.

I was happy with the refund. I was pleased to have successfully field-tested another technique. I was also fair: the next day, I posted a new message, acknowledging Ventura's correction of the problem.

FIVE TECHNIQUES FOR DEALING WITH BIG BUSINESSES

F aceless corporations—those companies that claim to care about their customers but refuse to take care of them when there's a problem—strike fear in the hearts of many consumers. They herd us into voice mail oblivion, fine-print us into a powerless corner, and EULA-gize us into signing away rights we don't know we have. Of course, we now know why they do it. A customer who reports a problem—is a problem customer. It costs less to replace one, than to deal with one. *It's just business.*

That's the beauty of the Unscrewed techniques for dealing with misbehaving monoliths. We make it all about business: their bottom line, their public image, and their viability in the marketplace. When we speak with them in their terms, and present them with a clear-cut financial decision, they will almost always make the right decision: to give you what you are due.

STUPID BUSINESS DECISIONS ARE MADE EVERY DAY

Very rarely will you run across a truly evil corporation, one that purposely mistreats its customers just because it can. Most often, the mistreatment is the result of corporate bureaucracy gone loony. This happened in the Unscrewed True Story "The Pee Doctors": a zero tolerance policy was applied without thought or logical review.

Throughout the years, much of the corporate world has become dependent on "MacWorkers," who act from a strict set of rules and read replies from a script. Because companies control their costs by hiring and firing according to that quarter's bottom line, it's not possible for them to have a highly skilled set of customer service representatives. In the Unscrewed True Story "The Unfriendly Skies," there was no way for Kevin, the customer service representative, to make a decision outside of the guidelines set forth on his screen or in his binder. The argument presented about saving his company money was entirely logical, but he was, by company policy, prevented from taking that into account. Kevin made a stupid business decision.

Millions of similar decisions are made every day by millions of corporate minions. They can't help it. The employees—particularly in Customer Support—have no authority to think outside the box, even if it will save the company money, time, or its reputation. Their job performance often is measured according to how well they implement the policies—however illogical—rather than how many customers they actually help, or how much money they save the company.

When I Unscrew one of these situations, I often close the conversation with a suggestion that the employee bring up the problem at the next departmental meeting. Many have acknowledged the illogic, unfairness, or even absurdity of a policy, but not once have I been told, "Great idea. I certainly will." Absent significant motivation, few are willing to step out of the box that has been built for them.

KNOCKING DOWN THE WALLS OF THE BOX

Most of the techniques used to Unscrew big business work by somehow forcing a customer service representative or sales employee to think outside the box. These low-paid employees are used to sheeplike customers doing exactly what they are told, accepting the "It's our policy" answer, and going away. Therefore, they are caught entirely by surprise when you say, "No, I will not do what you ask. You will not put me on hold. I do not accept the premise that your internal policies have anything to do with my expectations of proper customer service."

They will do their best to herd you along until you are "fleeced" at the end. Other than the obligatory first call to Customer Service—just to make sure the employees aren't the good guys—the Unscrewed techniques for dealing with big business are all about keeping you out of the herd of sheep and keeping them on their toes.

WITH BIG BUSINESS, IT'S BACKWARD

When dealing with small business, you walk up to—or call up—the decision maker and tell that person what's about to happen if he or she doesn't take care of you. With big business, getting to the decision maker is often the hard part. We've often got to demonstrate our leverage *prior* to actually talking with the decision maker. Therefore, with many of the big-business techniques, the steps are these:

1. Do something to get their attention.
2. Negotiate.

Once you've demonstrated the tenacity required to get them on the line, they will often quickly come to terms on an acceptable goal.

JUST THE FACTS, MA'AM

Whereas a small businessperson may be your neighbor and you are likely to have occasional interactions with him or her, the person at the other end of the corporate call is anonymous, and you are nothing but a number. She does not care about your story, your hardship, your pain, your suffering, what trouble the company may have caused you, or even whether you are going to continue to be a customer. She assumes that you won't. Her job is to mitigate the damage, paying you as little as she can to make you go away, quietly.

When dealing with a big business, have all the facts at hand: the dates of any contracts, phone calls, letters, e-mails, and so on. Have the names and titles of anyone you have spoken with previously. Of course, always get the information on every person who is on the other end of your call. When you tell your story, keep it short and pertinent to the situation.

"I purchased your Typhoon Plus Mark IV vacuum on December 30. At 10:15 a.m. Pacific Standard Time on January 11, I contacted Customer Service. I waited on hold for eighteen minutes. I spoke with Lara Baker, agent number A56498, mother of two—Jason, who is five, and Mary, who is eight—in the Phoenix call center. She assured me that a replacement unit would be shipped to my home the next business day via two-day express. That was eight days ago."

I'm not telling the representative that my carpet is dirty, that I'm having a big dinner party that night and need a vacuum, or that I'm really pissed off that either the agent lied to me or the company is so screwed up it can't do something as simple as shipping a vacuum cleaner on the right date. Take notice of the detail. When faced with that kind of record keeping, a customer service representative is left with little wiggle room. It's hard to deny that you spoke with Lara, particularly because you know her kids' ages. The only question at this point is whether the failure is the result of deceit or incompetence.

Of course, if every situation were that easy to wrap up and tie with a bow, we wouldn't need the Unscrewed Solution. The biggest difference between dealing with big business and individuals or small companies is getting someone simply to pay attention. That's why three of the five following techniques for big business—"Faxing For Dollars," "The Online Critique," and "The Financial Pages"—are really just door openers. Once you're on the inside, you will speak either with a reasonable individual who will understand the Unscrewed cost equation or with someone who doesn't understand but upon whom you can work one of the other business techniques.

BIG-BUSINESS TECHNIQUE NUMBER ONE: 800 CASH CALL

Type: Telephone.

Upside: Immediate response, cost to company is immediate.

Downside: Very aggressive approach, which can incite negative reaction.

Props & Tools: Telephone, computer with modem.

"800 Cash Call" is a way of attracting the attention of a company that is trying very hard to ignore you, or has outright told you to just go away. It is a very aggressive technique, to be used when you feel that none of the other more mild-mannered techniques will prove effective. You may recall that I used this technique in the Unscrewed True Story "The Shady Auto Shipper." Some of my seminar attendees have also used it effectively when dealing with travel agencies, stock brokerages, and even telemarketers; all you need is a toll-free number to call.

The Unscrewed Promise for "800 Cash Call"

"Mr. Steele, I'm glad I finally got you on the phone. I have been unable to resolve a simple issue [*briefly describe it*] with your company, which could easily be solved by [*your acceptable goal*]. Accordingly, I feel compelled to do whatever I can to protect my fellow citizens from your unfair and unethical business practices.

"I imagine that your phone lines will be so tied up for the next twenty-four hours that you will not be making a lot of sales. It might not get me what I'm due, but I will feel much better knowing that you have been unable to take advantage of another unsuspecting customer.

"Please use the time to reconsider how you have dealt with my particular situation. When you are ready to discuss this matter with me further, I can be reached at [*your phone number*] or by e-mail [*in case your phone line is tied up*]."

After this, the one who speaks first, loses.

Let's take a look at this technique, sentence by sentence and paragraph by paragraph.

Paragraph 1: "Mr. Steele…business practices."

You are stating your case, and reminding him of your acceptable goal. You are also stating your motive for acting. You are not seeking revenge; you are trying to protect others from meeting the same fate as you.

Paragraph 2: "I imagine…another unsuspecting customer."

You are letting him know what to expect, and then stating that, for you, money is not the object. (Once again, this is the difference between what we say and what our goal truly is.)

Paragraph 3: "Please use the…or by e-mail."

You are letting him know that you are still open for negotiation and how he may get in touch with you.

This technique is a two-for-one—meaning that it hurts your opponent in two ways. It costs the company money in the form of toll-free number charges, and it ties up the phone lines for incoming sales. This technique is most effective when dealing with a medium to large company that depends on toll-free phone lines for incoming sales calls. Every time the company's toll-free number is called, it costs the company money (anywhere from 30¢ to more than $1).

The principle is simple. Program your computer modem to dial the company's toll free number for incoming sales, and to keep dialing until it makes a connection to a computer—which it never will. Usually, this is as simple as setting the "number of attempts" option in the modem settings to some ridiculously high number: 10,000 works well. Your computer will call the sales line; a salesperson will answer and hang up. Your computer will try again; a salesperson will answer and hang up. Your computer will try again—you get the idea. The computer keeps dialing in hopes of finding another computer, and then a person answers. (*How stupid can these humans be?* it thinks.)

The company may ask the phone company to block your number. If you have a second line, use that. If you are using a laptop, carry it to a friend's house and use your friend's line. If you have friends with computers willing to help in the project, that's great, too. It usually doesn't take long before the decision makers at the company realize that they are losing sales and spending a lot of valuable time dealing with you, and that they would be better off just settling with you.

This is a very aggressive technique, and it can get people upset. Therefore, when you finally receive "the phone call," you should be doubly careful to be calm and businesslike. "I realize my techniques may be a bit hardball, Mr. Steele. I just believe so strongly in a consumer's right to be treated fairly. I'm glad we can reach an agreement on this. Thank you."

This is the only technique where the business losses are instantaneous and measurable—in the form of the cost of the toll-free number calls. You must make sure that at no time do you state that "losing business or costing you money on your toll-free number lines" is your objective. Even though you know that is the financial cattle prod of this technique, you can never state this.

By the way, the "thank you" at the close doesn't hurt anything, and it can help a lot. You may be steaming. However, a small statement of gratitude at the end of the conversation can help assuage any remaining anger on your opponent's side, thereby making the company more likely to fulfill its part of the negotiation.

BIG-BUSINESS TECHNIQUE NUMBER TWO: FAXING FOR DOLLARS

Type: Telephone, fax.

Upside: Immediate response.

Downside: Slightly aggressive approach, which may be read as "a little crazy."

Props & Tools: Telephone, fax machine or computer with fax capability.

As stated, the most difficult part of getting what you deserve from a large company is just getting the company's attention. It is often impossible to find a living, breathing human being at the end of some branch of the voice mail maze. Even when you do, that person is probably unable to provide a solution to your problem.

"Faxing for Dollars" is a technique that I have used successfully for many years to attract the attention of the decision makers in Sales and Customer Service Departments and at the highest levels of corporations. Unlike many of the techniques, where you use a phone to state your case, explain your motivation, and present your acceptable goal, with this technique, that is all done in a fax that you send to every available phone number within the executive offices of the company that you're dealing with.

The letter should be clear and unemotionally state your case. Make the point that you have already attempted to go through the regular customer service channels and that you are resorting to contacting them in this manner only because you "have been unable to reach a mutually acceptable resolution to this matter through traditional channels." The language may seem a bit formal, but it is code language that tells the people at the top that you understand the process and have gone through it. Don't forget to put in your contact information: telephone and e-mail. Have someone double-check the letter for grammar and spelling. (Everyone needs an editor, even writers of consumer self-help books.)

Major corporations don't generally list their internal fax numbers on their web site or billing statements. However, you can often find them with a few minutes of research on the Internet. Executive Office, Sales Department, and other internal fax numbers can be found in a surprising number of documents. Here's what to search for:

- Financial documents, which are often found in the Investor Relations section.
- Press releases.
- Promotional materials for internal events, such as golf tournaments and holiday parties.
- Sales materials.
- Contracts and other legal documents.

It's amazing how easy it can be to find these internal numbers. On a search engine, I once found the home fax number of the president of a Fortune 500 company. It was provided on a church contact list; turns out he was secretary of the church board.

Even if you are unable to locate the Executive Office's fax number on the Internet, it is often surprisingly easy to call the company's main switchboard and ask for it. You must have the right reason for requesting it, though. The switchboard operator won't give it out to just anybody.

"I'm with the firm of Burley & Burley. I've got a balance sheet that I'm supposed to fax to Ms. Jones's office, but all I have is the district fax number, and I certainly don't want to send it there." (This implies a high level of confidentiality.) Even at this point, don't directly ask for the Executive Office's fax number; it will be offered freely. If it isn't, then ask for it. However, receptionists are often so wary of that request that it sets off alarm bells.

Here's another approach.

"Hi. Ms. Ramona Jones requested a list of tee times for October. She didn't give me a fax number to send it to. Can you help me?" Once again, don't specifically ask for the fax number. The question is implied. What counts here is the apparently mundane and unthreatening nature of the request.

After you have uncovered as many fax numbers as possible at the highest levels of the organization, fax them all identical copies of your well-written letter—again and again—until you get a response, which should be quickly.

With a standard fax machine, you may end up standing over it for an hour or so. Grab yourself a cup of coffee or juice and enjoy the break. With a computer fax, you can easily enter all the numbers into the computer and send the fax to that address list. Just send the same fax several dozen times. Depending on the number of fax numbers you were able to uncover, each machine should be affected by your efforts every five to ten minutes.

Once again, when you receive the phone call from the vice president of Customer Relations or the regional director of Sales, stay calm and businesslike. You are in charge of the situation; the executive is responding to you.

"Thank you for calling. I realize that you are a very busy person, so I hope that we can come to a quick resolution of this matter."

The executive may have assumed that you are a crazy person or a zealot; just show her that you are sane, that your request is reasonable, and that all you want is your acceptable goal. She will quickly do the math and realize that it is in the company's best interests—in time, effort, and energy—just to take care of you, whether or not she believes that you are right. It's called "paying you to go away."

BIG-BUSINESS TECHNIQUE NUMBER THREE: THE FINANCIAL PAGES

Type: Internet.
Upside: Very public, quick response.
Downside: Ineffective with privately held companies.
Props & Tools: Internet-equipped computer.

Many companies, particularly in the technology and communications industries, are driven by their stock price. The decisions they make on a day-to-day basis are based more on how the ticker will be affected than the revenues for the quarter. (Hardly anybody cares about *annual* sales numbers anymore.)

If the nemeses are part of the technology or communications industry, then the fastest way to attract their attention may be to have an impact on what *they* consider to be most important, which is not the bottom line but the price of their stock. Although most of us do not have the financial clout or investment industry influence to affect a company's share price, there are methods an individual can use to have an impact, such as the technique that I applied to attract the attention of the online travel agent in the Unscrewed True Story "The Terrible Travel Agency."

There are several key financial web sites on the Internet. Two of the most popular sites are CBS MarketWatch and Yahoo! Finance. Go to either of these sites, and enter the stock symbol for the company you are dealing with. For example, Microsoft's stock symbol is MSFT. Just type this into the quote box, and it will take you to a page full of information about Microsoft. On that page, you will also find the investor message board. This is where the Unscrewing begins.

These message boards are often the dark dungeons of financial dialogue, full of pitch people, con artists, sales-people, and other questionable types. There are also messages from stockholders, asking questions about the company, its finances, and its future. This is why most companies have at least one person on staff whose job is to pay attention to what people are saying in the online message rooms.

To implement this technique, you will post a message in your adversary's financial forum. It will have the following elements:

1. You have been a longtime customer. This is always true. Just how long is "longtime"? For some people, an hour in a boring classroom is an eternity. For a mistreated customer, a day is decades. You are always a "longtime" customer.
2. You have recently been mistreated. Describe it briefly, pointing out how easy it would be for the company to sat-isfy you if their policies didn't get in the way and they just had a little more common sense.
3. You are taking your business elsewhere. State that you know of other longtime customers of the company who are also jumping ship. Regretfully state that "it is a shame that such a great company has fallen into decline so quickly."
4. Include your contact phone number or e-mail. Leaving this information proves that you are a genuine customer, not someone just trying to push the stock price. If you are a regular customer, the company will likely have your contact information from billing, purchase, or customer service records. In the event the company does not have

that information, it will give them a way to contact you. Be wise about where and when you give out your phone number and e-mail address. You should provide it to only the company web site or company-sponsored forum. Revealing this information on other public web sites or chat rooms can leave you wide open to telephone solicitors or e-mail spammers.

Investors fear financial surprises. If a company is failing fast, they do not want to be the last to hear the news. That would mean a steep decline in stock price. They all have their fingers to the wind, looking for trends. A potential decline in consumer confidence in a company is a strong wind indeed.

The company watchers know this and will respond quickly to stifle a cool wind from the wrong direction. If your lament brings out a few others, and that spooks a handful of speculative investors, the stock price could fall. I'm not saying that your single letter is going to bring down Microsoft, but let's put some math to it.

As of the date of this writing, Microsoft's per-share stock price was $25.53. There were 10,710,000,000 shares in the hands of stockholders, making the net worth roughly $273,426,300,000. If your little letter caused the stock price to drop just one penny to $25.52 per share, the net worth would fall to $273,319,200,000—a loss of $107 million.

So when you receive the call from the vice president of Customer Relations, remain calm and businesslike. Briefly tell your story, state your acceptable goal, and be quiet. He will comply. The company cannot afford not to.

BIG-BUSINESS TECHNIQUE NUMBER FOUR: THE ONLINE CRITIQUE

Type: Internet.

Upside: Very public; moderate response time.

Downside: Reviews and critiques may be edited, pertains to retail products only.

Props & Tools: Internet-equipped computer.

"The Online Critique" is very similar to "The Financial Pages," except that it is designed for companies that are more in touch with their retail sales numbers than their stock ticker.

Companies that manufacture consumer products—for example, home electronics, appliances, housewares, or children's products—are most susceptible to this technique. More than advertising, they depend upon word of mouth to generate sales. The success of Apple's iPod music player wasn't the result of a clever advertising campaign. It caught on because one person told another, who told another, and because others wrote online reviews that were seen by thousands. Eventually, the mass media started paying attention.

The retail strength of Amazon.com and similar online retailers is what makes this technique possible. Online retailers have become huge customers for manufacturers of everything from books to baby toys. Many of them, including Amazon, allow customers to write online critiques of the products they have purchased. You can rate your experience with the product according to a certain number of stars and even write a several-hundred-word review, telling the good, the bad, and the "faulty." (I used this technique in the Unscrewed True Story "The Printer Maker.")

Here's how you carry out this technique:

1. Use a natural writing voice. You are writing to fellow consumers, not a business. You want to sound approachable, like a real person. This *is* the time to share emotional horror stories about how that camera failed to catch that "once-in-a-lifetime" picture of your baby's first steps. Or how the coffeemaker exploded and nearly blinded your precious four-year-old daughter. Don't get bogged down in detail, but make sure you pull at the heartstrings.

2. Show how you have been fair. Describe how you have made every attempt to work with the company, but that it has been surprisingly unhelpful and unresponsive. Give details about phone calls, the terribly long wait on hold

with that horrible music, and so on. Keep the language clean and reasonable. You want to sound like a second-grade teacher from the Midwest: an intelligent, middle-class person who is simply trying to get what is right from a company that is doing you wrong.

3. Make a strong recommendation. Do not pull any punches. The online critics' points are averaged. If you rate the company as 0 or 1 (1 is the lowest on some sites), you are going to stand out and cause a drop in the average. Companies have watchers on these sites, too, and they will pay attention.

4. Include contact information. (But note that if you are confident that your customer record is on file with the company or their Customer Service Department, it is not necessary to include your contact information.) Sometimes the online store will not allow you to include this information. On other sites, you can check a box, giving the site permission to provide your contact information to the company.

Although this technique usually has a moderate response time, in some cases, the response is immediate. Manufacturers can track their online sales in real time. If you write a scathing online review and the sales numbers start dipping, a manufacturer or distributor is going to want to know why, and want to do something about it immediately.

On the other hand, with some companies it could be several days before they notice your review. They might even dismiss it. If more than a week has passed without a call or an e-mail, consider using another technique.

However, when you do get that phone call, stay calm. Restate your acceptable goal and stick to it. They will usually agree quickly. After all, you're just one purchaser, and your review could be turning away hundreds. They may request that you update your online review. That is not unreasonable. However, update the critique only *after* you have received satisfaction from your adversary.

BIG-BUSINESS TECHNIQUE NUMBER FIVE:
MR. STOCKHOLDER

Type: Telephone, Internet.

Upside: Extraordinarily quick response.

Downside: Ineffective with privately held companies.

Props & Tools: Telephone, Internet-equipped computer, online brokerage account.

"Buy-Bye Customers" is my favorite Unscrewed technique, but "Mr. Stockholder" comes in a close second.

For years, I contemplated how a little person could have a real impact on a Fortune 500 company. Sure, if the company watches its stock prices, "The Financial Pages" works great. However, some companies don't care about their minute-by-minute stock price, and their retail products are not sold on Yahoo! or Amazon. For the longest time, they appeared unassailable—until the day I was struck with the epiphany of "Mr. Stockholder."

First, log into your online brokerage account. If you don't have one, you can easily get one. Go online to eTrade.com or Ameritrade.com. You can open an account with a credit card. There are no setup fees. You can usually get started in a matter of minutes. Your first equity purchase will be between one and ten shares of your adversary's stock. When your transaction is complete, call the Investor Relations phone number listed on the company's web site.

The Unscrewed Promise for "Mr. Stockholder"

"Ms. James, I am a stockholder of XYZ Corporation because I believe in the quality of our service, our product, our employees, and, above all, how we treat our customers. Therefore, I was completely astonished when my own XYZ product failed, and I was given the runaround by Customer Service. All I had asked for was [*your acceptable goal*].

"I believe that if President Merritt-Willingham knew that we were treating our customers this way, he'd send some heads rolling. I think it will also be important for the other stockholders to know that something has happened to our company that we have placed so much faith in. The situation is so distressing that this year I have decided not to release my vote to proxy. Instead, I am going to take advantage of my right as a stockholder to address the board personally at our annual meeting."

After this, the one who speaks first, loses.

Let's take a look at this technique, sentence by sentence and paragraph by paragraph.

Paragraph 1, Sentence 1: "Ms. James…treat our customers."

You are firmly establishing yourself as a proud and loyal stockholder. These people are her responsibility.

Paragraph 1, Sentences 2 and 3: "Therefore, I was…[*your acceptable goal*]."

You are now letting her know that the problem is actually fairly easy to fix. It's not a matter of an investor lawsuit: all you want is a replacement XYZ product or refund. At this point, she is relieved.

Paragraph 2: "I believe that if…at our annual meeting."

You have created a nightmare scenario. Ms. James, vice president of Investor Relations, doesn't want some hick-from-the-sticks showing up in the middle of their well-choreographed and expensive corporate annual meeting. Some corporations don't actually let stockholders stand at a microphone and address the board, though many do. You could easily substitute handing out flyers in the lobby of the hotel where the meeting is being held. The promise of any disturbance is certain to send Ms. James hurrying down the hall to find out what the Customer Service Department could have possibly done to one of her stockholders to make him so upset that he would actually want to *appear* before the board.

The success of this technique depends on your ability to convince Ms. James that you are bound-and-determined to tell your story to the board of directors. You may want to research when the actual meeting will be held, and where. Make a room reservation: you can always cancel it with twenty-four hours' notice at no charge. You could even look into airline flights. "I would like to ask you something, Ms. James. I see that I can catch either the Delta or the American flight into Atlanta.

Which airline do you recommend?" These little touches will absolutely convince her that you will arrive in person in the middle of the meeting—and that will not be good.

This technique combines the audacity of "Just a Little Bit Jack" with the potential stock downside of "The Financial Pages." Not only stockholders attend those meetings—stock analysts do, too. They also listen in on conference calls. If just one of them were to lose faith in XYZ Corporation and drop his or her rating, the potential downside for the company could be in the millions of dollars.

UNSCREWED TRUE STORY

The Monitor Manufacturer

Everyone has their dream "thing." One person might want a black sports car. Someone else might ogle a baby blue iPod. At one time, for me, it was a flat-screen twenty-inch computer monitor. I'd been using my old fifteen-inch monitor for many years. The colors were fading, and the Microsoft Windows task bar was permanently burned into the bottom of the screen.

I finally decided that I'd get it for myself—for my birthday. It was an expensive gift, more than $700. Two days after ordering it online, my new Toyo monitor arrived via express courier. I carefully unpacked it and placed it in the center of my desktop. That monitor was a thing of beauty. It made my work so much easier, too. I was able to see two pages side by side on the huge screen.

Three weeks later, I walked into my home office to get started on my workday. I pushed the button on the power strip to energize my workstation, and I heard a quiet *pop*, followed by a sickening electrical smell. It took only a moment of sniffing to figure out that the odor was coming from deep within my new monitor. My beautiful new twenty-inch flat-screen monitor…was dead.

I didn't even call Customer Service right away. I had a cup of black coffee on the back deck while I mourned the loss of my big screen. After quickly passing through the five stages of grief, I called the Toyo Customer Service line. It is a big company. The voice mail maze was intimidating. Once the company confirmed that I was a residential consumer of computer products and was seeking technical repair support on a video monitor, I was told that my wait would be no longer than thirteen minutes.

Twenty-five minutes later, a voice interrupted a violin instrumental version of Led Zeppelin's "Stairway to Heaven."

"Toyo Technical Support. My name's Sean. How can I help you?"

He sounded really bored. I told him my story.

"Is it still under warranty?" he asked.

"I'd hope so," I said. "It's less than a month old."

There was a long silence, as if he were waiting for me to say something more. I finally did.

"So what do I need to do to get a new monitor?"

"Do you still have the original box?" he asked. I did.

"You need to pack it up and ship it to our California Service Center. I'll give you a return merchandise authorization number."

"Can't I get a replacement?" I asked. "I mean, it's less than a month old and—"

"No," Sean said, cutting me off. "If you were a corporate customer, we could trans-ship, but we don't do that with residential customers. Repair will decide whether it's a warranty issue and whether it should be fixed or replaced. They'll give you a call."

This was early on in my understanding of the Unscrewed principles, and I didn't realize that I could change the rules. I dutifully wrote down the return merchandise authorization (RMA) number that Sean gave me.

"Thanks for your help," I said, and hung up. An express courier picked up the monitor that afternoon. I paid extra for overnight service. With luck, I might have it back within a few days.

Two weeks later, I'd not heard a thing from the Toyo Repair Center. I decided to call them directly.

"You need to be going through our Customer Service Department," said a tech named Oscar.

"No, they said that you would call me as soon as you had received and diagnosed the problem with my monitor. I never got a call."

"Oh," Oscar said. "What was the RMA number?"

I told him and was not pleased with his response. "We never received it."

"Yes, you did," I said, giving him the tracking number and the name of the person who the shipping company records showed had signed for it.

"Yeah, that's one of our dock guys," Oscar replied, sounding puzzled. "Let me take your number and I'll get back to you."

Stunned by the fact that my monitor had not been repaired yet, but, in fact, was lost within their system, I stammered, "Sure, call me back as soon as you can."

That turned out to be three days.

"Good news!" Oscar said. "We found your monitor. All we can figure is that a lot of stuff came in that day and it was put on the side. Nobody noticed it sitting there, so it never got entered into the system."

"So what's the status now?" I asked.

"A technician put it on the bench and ran some checks. It's got internal damage."

"Sounds bad," I lamented. "How long will it take you to fix it? It was lost for a while, so can you put a rush on it?"

"That's up to you," Oscar said. "Internal damage isn't covered by warranty. The repair estimate is $834."

I couldn't believe what I was hearing.

"What kind of internal damage are you talking about?"

"Doesn't say," Oscar replied. "But you sent it in for repair, so it couldn't have been okay."

"I didn't send it in because it had been damaged. It just died."

"It could have happened during shipment to us."

"Does the shipping record show any damage to the box? Is there any damage to the outside of the monitor?"

"No, I was there when they opened it. From the outside, the shipping carton and the monitor both look fine."

"So what you're telling me is that—somehow during shipping—the monitor suffered severe internal damage, but there is no sign of it on either the plastic case or the double-padded shipping box."

"Yes, that's right."

"No, that's not right."

I think Oscar was insulted. "Just let us know what you want to do," he said, and hung up.

Something had to be done.

I knew that although it was a big corporation, Toyo was a latecomer to the market in computer monitors. It had been making a big push to catch up. Its precarious market position provided the inspiration for how I could Unscrew the situation.

Ten minutes of cruising the Toyo corporate pages—on my old, tired, fifteen-inch monitor—revealed the fax number for the vice president of Sales for Toyo America. I wrote up "The Story of the Monitor" and drafted a cover letter. At 11 a.m., I faxed it…twelve times.

The "story" was a play-by-play record of the monitor history and my experience with the Toyo America Customer Service Department. The cover letter read as follows:

To Whom This May Concern:

Please read the attached story carefully. I'm sure you
will find it as absurd as I do, particularly when I am
being asked to pay a repair bill that exceeds the price
that I paid for the product in the first place. The illogic is
exceeded only by the audacity of the request.

I am not going to pay to repair the monitor. Instead, I
am going to pass out copies of my story to every customer entering my nearest Computer Universe store. I
know that it may do nothing to get my monitor repaired,
but I feel that I have a responsibility to let as many people as I can know about your irresponsible technical
support practices. I'm also going to make sure that the
store manager knows exactly why I'm standing out front,
making customers go away.

Regretfully from one of your former loyal customers,

Ron Burley

I never heard one word from the Toyo Executive Offices
or the Repair Center. However, the following morning, a
brand-new twenty-inch Toyo monitor arrived on my doorstep.

THREE TECHNIQUES FOR DEALING WITH THE GOVERNMENT AND MEGACORPORATIONS

When dealing with the government, the basic principle of the Unscrewed Solution gets tossed out the back window of a racing Humvee. "It's all about the money" doesn't apply when dealing with the people who print currency, or who store it in cargo containers, or who can tap your wallet for more whenever they need it.

It's this absence of monetary motivation that can make governmental agencies among the most intractable, annoying, and unresponsive organizations you'll ever deal with. From the Department of Motor Vehicles to the Department of Defense, you're unlikely to come across a more entrenched group of employees, policies, and traditions.

These traits can also be found in some of the largest megacorporations—the kind with gross annual revenues greater than all of Scandinavia. Therefore, when I refer to "the government" in this chapter, you can also think *megacorporation*. The employees in megacorporations are protected by some of the same shields as government employees, making them immune to some Unscrewed techniques that will work with employees of smaller companies. In both cases, employees can only be fired under specific, limited circumstances. Unfortunately, employees of megacorporations and the government often suffer from acute apathy regarding the operating efficiency or public image of their employer. They live within an employment fortress protected by rules, union agreements, and tradition, and are often out of touch with the actual purpose of their company or agency: taking care of their customers or constituents.

A classic example of how a government agency can lose touch with its mission occurred during the Hurricane Katrina disaster that ravaged the Southeast United States in the summer of 2005. The government agency responsible for responding to the emergency—the Federal Emergency Management Agency (FEMA)—appeared more concerned with image than with actually providing assistance to people in need. To be fair, in that case, the cancer started at the top. There were legions of mid-level FEMA employees who still cared a great deal, even though the leadership failed in its mission. FEMA's behavior in that disaster does bring out a good point; in many cases, the culture of complacency begins at the top and customer-contact employees are just the most visible part of a diseased corporate or government culture.

Forty years earlier, consumer crusader Ralph Nader uncovered the epitome of corporate disinterest and misplaced priorities in his landmark book called *Unsafe at Any Speed*. Nader and his team of researchers revealed that American automakers had made a deal with the devil, sacrificing driver and passenger safety in the pursuit of greater profits.

In one case, Ford Motor Company's mainstream compact, the Pinto, had a nasty habit of exploding into a ball of fire after relatively slow-speed crashes. Tests demonstrated that the Pinto's unprotected and low-slung gas tank was particularly vulnerable to rear-end impacts. Digging deeper, Nader's "Raiders" discovered that Ford had known about the Pinto's problems for several years. Instead of fixing the trouble, Ford executives decided the more profitable path would be to pay damages that might arise from lawsuits rather than to commit to a costly redesign of the vehicle. In his book, *The End of Detroit*, author Micheline Maynard points to the "Big Three" automakers' disregard of customer safety as a major factor in the decline of the American auto industry.

LIFERS BY CHOICE

Within the legions of government workers, or within the ranks of megacorporations, are a special breed of employees: the "lifers." These employees value security above all else. They know their date of retirement and the amount of their pension check, to the penny. Lifers pose problems for us. They don't really care about the bottom line. They are immune from most financial pressures—protected by union rules, company policies, and regulatory edict.

When I've been screwed by the government, it has most often been in the form of a mistake it has made and is unwilling to correct. Or, if it is willing to make things right, the timeline for action is measured in terms of continental drift.

Without the financial crowbar to wave over the heads of these bunkered bureaucrats, what can we do to get Unscrewed? That question challenged my efforts for several years. As situations came up, I tried a number of techniques. Most of them failed.

The answer to this perplexing problem finally came to me one morning in Honolulu, while I was waiting to meet with a member of the city council for an interview. I watched a stream of workers flow into the concrete bastions of government. As the procession passed in front of me, I came to understand a basic truth about government and megacorporation employees: the last thing they want is notoriety. Their fantasy future depends upon them showing up at their job on time, doing it within defined and contracted parameters, and staying out of trouble.

TROUBLE WITH A CAPITAL T

Trouble—in the institutional employment pool—can be defined as anything that forces an employee to do something out of the ordinary. If your job is keeping track of office supplies and you forget to order copy paper, you'll get a demerit on your job evaluation form. Forget to initial the annual audited restatement of interdepartmental equipment transfers, and you'll get a demerit. Create extra work for any other employee—particularly your immediate superior—and you'll get several demerits on your performance record.

At regular intervals, those demerits are tallied up. Too many and that precious timeline may need adjustment. Gold stars don't seem to be given out for good work. Apparently, most institutional and governmental employee programs are punitive, rather than supportive—which explains a lot about why we have the type of government institutions that we do.

There is one thing even worse than the dreaded demerits. If you are a government or megacorporation employee and somehow attract negative high-level or public attention for your department or your boss, you are all but guaranteed to stay in your current cubicle for the rest of your career. Your precious promotion timeline is toast. Such situations have driven more than one government lifer to grab an official inventoried dull-edged letter opener with the intention of ending it all.

The employee grading system is one of the levers you will use to get some movement out of a government lifer.

VIOLATING OUR OWN RULES

My moment of clarity about public employees led to a startling twist in applying the Unscrewed Solution. When dealing with businesses, we work very hard to make sure that our negotiations are completely impersonal. When dealing with the government and similar institutions, however, our approach must be absolutely personal. The unspoken message that you send to the government employee is that he or she has a choice. *What will it be? A bright and cozy future? Or a hopeless eternity in endless drudgery?*

Warning: Be *very* careful about how you apply the pressure. Even someone at the lowest government pay grade can have the ability to completely mess with your life. A misplaced file, a mistyped account number and before you can say, "Guess I goofed," the IRS is on your doorstep and the sheriff is holding a foreclosure auction.

Dealing with the government is always a serious matter. It is, inevitably, time-consuming. Your Unscrewed Plan cost equation can go out the window if you have to stand in line just once at a government office.

When dealing with the government, record keeping is more important than in any other negotiation. Be absolutely meticulous about what was said, who said it, and when it was said. If possible, use the "This may be taped for training purposes" disclaimer to get all conversations on tape or on your hard drive. Burn them to a CD and keep them for ten years.

When dealing with government issues, there might be no dollar amount involved, just a situation that must be resolved. The goal is to come to a resolution of the problem as quickly and efficiently as possible, limiting your cost in time, effort, and lost income as much as possible.

GOVERNMENT TECHNIQUE NUMBER ONE: HEAD ABOVE THE WALL/COCONSPIRATOR

Type: Telephone.

Upside: Works with low-level employees who have no loyalty or interest in the success of their agency or organization.

Downside: Could be seen as personal threat if not presented properly.

Props & Tools: Telephone.

Imagine legions of government employees in their cubicles, stretching on for miles in every direction. All you can see is the wisps of thinning hair occasionally wafting above the edge of the carpeted dividers. The manager of these minions is standing next to you with a club, ready to play whack-a-mole with any employee whose head appears above the wall.

After you have done your research regarding the organization, you can place your call.

The Unscrewed Promise for "Head Above the Wall/Coconspirator"

"Milly, thank you for taking my call this afternoon. I appreciate the hard work that all of you do in [*agency name*]. I am attempting to straighten out a situation [*tell your story briefly, including what error has occurred*]. All that I'm looking for is [*your acceptable goal*].

"I'm going to be faxing a letter to Director Adamson's office this afternoon, letting him know how we've been able to resolve this situation.

"Milly, I know that you're not responsible for what has happened up to this point, and would probably prefer not to be dealing with it. However, the fates have brought you and me together today, so let's make the most of it. Of course, your name will be prominently featured in the first paragraph of the letter that lands on the director's desk. You sound like a very nice person; I'm rooting for you to be the hero of the story, rather than the villain.

"I know that you can see how this situation isn't fair. I believe that there's got to be some way that two intelligent people such as you and me—working together—can make the system work reasonably well for everyone. Let's do it. OK?"

After this, the one who speaks first, loses.

Let's take a look at this technique, sentence by sentence and paragraph by paragraph.

Paragraph 1, Sentences 1 and 2: "Milly, thank you…[*agency name*]."

Government workers are rarely thanked for the work they do. This opening demonstrates that you are a compassionate person, who has at some point worked in government, has a relative who does, or is maybe even closely connected to a "higher-up."

Paragraph 1, Sentences 3 and 4: "I am attempting to…[*your acceptable goal*]."

State your problem as dispassionately and matter-of-factly as possible. Milly has heard the story a thousand times and has a pat answer to deal with it. You are also laying your acceptable goal on the table.

Paragraph 2: "I'm going to be faxing...resolve this situation."

You are implying that you have a personal relationship with the director of her agency. In this situation, I've earlier called the Director's Office and simply asked, "Would you be interested in getting a short note of feedback on your Customer Service team?" They inevitably say yes. (Be sure to get the person's name you spoke with. You can also say, "Tiffany, in Director Adamson's office, is waiting for my fax to let her know how things turned out.")

Paragraph 3, Sentences 1 and 2: "Milly, I know...the most of it."

You are telling Milly that you have no hard feelings toward her and that you in no way blame her for any short-falls of the past. You are apologetic about putting her in the situation of having to deal with you. It is also a slight warning of what may happen if she doesn't pay attention.

Paragraph 3, Sentence 3: "Of course, your name...the director's desk."

This is the whack-a-mole club. Despite all previous assertions that you do not blame her, you are threatening to raise her head above the wall. The last thing she wants is for her name to be on the director's lips. She probably has never met the person and has hoped she never would until she receives her gold watch at retirement.

Paragraph 3, Sentence 4: "You sound like...the villain."

Not only is her name going to appear in a letter, but she could also end up being blamed for causing this situation to turn up as an annoyance on the director's desk. In government, as everywhere else, all brown stuff rolls downhill. By the time the fallout has slid the multiple levels to Milly's floor, it may have gained a lot of momentum. Every person along the line is going to be a little irritated for having to interrupt what he or she was doing in order to find out why some low-level worker couldn't properly handle a tax-paying constituent.

Paragraph 4: "I know that you…Let's do it."

There's a retail sales technique called coconspirator. The salesperson says something like, "My manager has said that we can't sell this for anything less than the sticker price. I really want to help you get this car. I know you love it, and you sure would look great in it. I know it's a bit more than your budget, but if you could come up with maybe $50 more on the monthly payment, I think I can convince him to give us a break. He might yell and scream—but we'll get him to see things our way. OK?" The principle of the coconspirator technique is that the salesperson steps over the line to become the ally of the customer, against the manager. Of course, it's an illusion, but just like the magician cutting the woman in half, it works. In Milly's case, you pull her over the line to work with you against the system that has frustrated her, and her callers, for years. You would be surprised by how willing many government employees are to step over that line. If you run into an agent who is not willing to play coconspirator, back out of the conversation and call back later to get another agent. Odds are, you'll find one willing to "do the right thing," to "join your team," even if it's just to relieve the boredom.

This Time, Keep It Personal

Every step of the way, remind Milly that she's going to be "Star for a Day" in that letter to the director. Although private industry management has realized the value of "positive strokes" for decades, government employees typically receive little positive recognition for their efforts. Take advantage of this.

Always keep that smile in your voice. Never be negative or threatening. With every little step forward in your negotiation, thank her and tell her, "That's the kind of stuff that's going to put a smile on the director's face, for sure." Let her know that she will be a hero, and that she is helping everyone in your family, including your three kids, "who are doing great in school, but it looks like the middle one will need braces."

The more you can make yourself a person to her, the more she will sympathize with you and become a willing participant in your efforts.

GOVERNMENT TECHNIQUE NUMBER TWO:
PRESS RELEASE PANDEMONIUM

Type: Telephone.

Upside: Works with higher-level employees and officials of local or regional agencies, who may be ambitious and therefore averse to negative publicity.

Downside: Could be time-consuming if you actually have to hold a press conference.

Props & Tools: Telephone, press release, media contact list (from phone book), striking visual items for media photo opportunities.

There are times when you end up speaking with the director, or other decision maker, of an agency. This person will listen intently, but in the end can be as unresponsive as anyone else. It's as if this individual were working in the private sector, rather than as a servant of the people. (By the way, it never helps to remind a civil servant that the taxpayers "pay your salary." Civil servants hear this so often that it is an annoyance.)

Although the director of an agency might be propelled into action when you use the "Head Above the Wall/Co-conspirator" technique, the odds are against it. This person's main concern is running a tight ship that stays within budget and doesn't earn negative headlines. It is this aversion to publicity that will work to your advantage.

Traditional consumer books might suggest that you write to whatever regulatory or oversight group is responsible for the agency. We know that takes far too long. A threat to send a letter to the oversight agency is likely to be met with a yawn or an outright suggestion to "go ahead." It is the public sector equivalent of calling Customer Service. It is the channel they want you to follow. The letter will land on a desk somewhere and get filed away into oblivion. You might receive a letter acknowledging receipt of your letter. Beyond that, the odds of someone actually taking action on or reviewing your complaint are probably less than winning the Powerball lottery. The only exception is if you are claiming that a crime has been committed. In that case, you should be contacting the county district attorney.

"Press Release Pandemonium" is similar to the "Sunday Supplement" technique recommended for small businesses, except that instead of creating a newspaper ad, you are going to create a press release to announce a press conference.

The press release might look something like this:

Southland Hills Citizens Association
Media Advisory
Wednesday, September 12, 2007

County Rejects Pleas from Southland Residents

The Canton County administration today rejected a plan to correct errors made in regard to local taxation and other financial matters for residents in the Southland Hills area. Press conference details:

> **Topic:** Southland Hills Taxation Errors
> **Date & Time:** Friday, September 14, 2007, 11:15 a.m.
> **Location:** 2598 South Hillsboro Avenue, Eugene, OR
> **Participants:** Ron Burley, Southland resident
> Mark Shine, Southland resident
> County Supervisor Blakemore (invited)
> **Visuals/Materials:** Additional information will be presented at the press conference. Southland residents and their children will be available for interviews. Media will also have access to Southland properties.

For more information, please contact:
Ron Burley
Office: 555-321-9876 Cell: 555-987-4321
E-mail: shca@ronburley.com

The press release should be all in one font without bold-face. No exclamation marks, condemnations, or defamatory rhetoric, which may offend the decision maker, is used. Keep it businesslike and factual. Few facts are mentioned in the release.

Certain elements of the press release are more important than others.

- Topic: Keep it short. Do not give away the whole story in the topic line. Otherwise, if you should actually hold the press conference, the media may not come, instead writing their stories just from the release. This is called press release journalism and will work against you in this case.
- Participants: Include the fact that the government official has been invited. That does not mean that this individual is expected. In fact, if the official doesn't show up, it will look as though this person is ducking the issue.
- Visuals: Television and print journalists love interviews and visuals. Letting them know that interview subjects will be available—particularly cute kids—is more important than it should be.

Of course, you don't want to be put in the position of actually sending out this press release to the media, or holding a press conference. However, your approach and manner must convince your adversary that you are absolutely serious about this. This is "fire for effect" at its finest. You do not intend to take the actions that will actually inflict damage on your opponent. Doing so would be too costly in time and treasure—even though your actions are absolutely intended to convince your adversary that you are willing to step up to the podium to share your story.

You are telling the decision maker that you are willing to make this very public, that you are willing to get the media involved, and that the decision maker will be forced into a public response—or, worse, a "no comment."

Locate the phone and fax number of the decision maker, using the same methods as in the business techniques. Fax the press release. Wait ten minutes and then place your phone call.

The Unscrewed Promise for "Press Release Pandemonium"

"Director Pappas, thank you for taking my call. I'm really disappointed that we've reached this point, when the situation could have been so easily handled by just [*your acceptable goal*].

"I sent you the press release to give you fair notice to adjust your schedule and prepare a response. I won't be releasing it until 4 p.m. this afternoon. I will follow up with the media to make sure they've received it and that we are on the rundown (the "rundown" is the lineup of news stories that will be covered in that broadcast).

"I'm sure you realize that government has been under fire recently for not being responsive to people's needs. This isn't as much about solving my situation as it is about doing my part as a concerned citizen in our community to point out that we need public officials who are responsive to their constituents."

After this, the one who speaks first, loses.

Let's take a look at this technique, sentence by sentence and paragraph by paragraph.

Paragraph 1, Sentences 1 and 2: "Director Pappas...[*your acceptable goal*]."

You are being a polite public citizen and showing respect for the director's position, even as you are lighting matches between his toes. You are also stating your acceptable goal in terms of "this is how to make me go away."

Paragraph 2, Sentence 1: "I sent you...a response."

You are demonstrating your basic fairness by giving him advance notice.

Paragraph 2, Sentence 2: "I won't be...this afternoon."

You are simultaneously showing your adversary that you understand the basic procedures of public relations and indirectly giving him his deadline for action.

Paragraph 3: "I'm sure you realize...their constituents."

You are giving him your talking points for the press conference. There's not much he can argue with when you state a desire for increased responsiveness by public officials.

If your acceptable goal is legal, and you have been treated unfairly, this technique can grease the wheels of government. Timelines fall by the wayside. Forms that were lost are quickly found. Inspectors who didn't have an open appointment for months show up on your doorstep within hours.

If your opponent does not respond to your first volley and you are actually forced to call a press conference, tell your story in as simple and personal terms as possible. The media are always interested in how big government is letting down the average person. I doubt that you'll have to face the cameras, though. I've used this technique at least a dozen times, and not once have I had to send out the press release.

GOVERNMENT TECHNIQUE NUMBER THREE: GOING TO THE TOP

Type: Telephone, fax.
Upside: Works with government employees at any level who are subject to regulatory or legislative oversight.
Downside: Response time can be slow.
Props & Tools: Telephone, fax machine.

There are times when traditional methods can have some value, but that doesn't mean that we have to go about them traditionally. Writing a complaint letter to a representative, senator, or regulatory official is a traditional solution, though most people go about it the wrong way.

The typical letter is a plea for help, telling a story of woe, rather than negotiating a position. "Going to the Top" means understanding how legislative and regulatory offices operate, and how you can make it easy for them to help you.

From mayor to president, all legislative and executive offices share the same concerns:

- How do we keep our jobs (meaning, how do we keep voter majority)?
- How do we prevent bad publicity and create good publicity?

- How do we create goodwill in the community that can be harvested at election time?

Whether sending it to a dogcatcher or a governor, your letter needs to address each of these points. Instead of writing a letter complaining about what has happened, your letter needs to focus on specific steps that can be taken to correct the situation, who needs to be contacted to make it happen, and an acceptable timeline. Also, mention the constituency or community affected.

Here is a sample letter:

Dear Commissioner Cullen:

For the past two years, our front yards have been flooded by spring rains. This has caused clogged storm drains in our area. We have called Director Jessup in the County Road Clearing Department (555-543-0987) and have been ignored. I have personally placed four calls on four separate days and have yet to receive a response. This is entirely unacceptable.

Based on expert examination of the problem, the entire project to clear the storm drains would take less than half a day.

We are looking to your office for support in resolving this matter. We voted for you in the most recent election. Although my neighbors and I have not been active in the political races for county commissioner in the past, how this matter is taken care of may inspire us to come out strongly—personally and financially—during the next election. I look forward to hearing from you.

Sincerely,

Ron Burley
Phone: 555-123-5678; Cell: 555-098-2345

There are three essential components of the letter. In the first paragraph, state the problem and the decision maker responsible—with contact information—for not taking action.

In the second paragraph, concisely state the solution you are seeking.

In the last paragraph, touch upon item number one in an elected official's list of priorities: your willingness to work for, or against, her in the next campaign.

In the example case, you would want to fax this letter simultaneously to Director Jessup (your adversary) and to Commissioner Cullen. In your own situation, some basic research will tell you who has authority over the department or agency that is giving you problems.

Do not expect a phone call from the elected official or head of the regulatory agency. If you get a call, it will likely be from an aide or assistant. Do not be offended. This is perfectly normal. If you do not receive a call within twenty-four hours, fax them again, and call ten minutes later. Legislative offices are often short on staff. Treat them as an ally helping you to solve the problem—while subtly reminding them of your willingness, based on the outcome, to use your personal and financial resources during the next election.

Not all government obstructionism is the result of entrenched bureaucracy or bad policies. Sometimes it's just a matter of plain old stupidity—as demonstrated in the next story.

UNSCREWED TRUE STORY

Battling the Bureaucrats

A few years ago, I earned my pilot's license. Flying is now my pastime. It is exhilarating to soar through the skies. It also helps me get around the country to do research for my various writing projects.

Last year, I finally scraped together enough cash to buy my own airplane. I spent several months looking in magazines and shopping local airports until I found just the right plane. It wasn't anything fancy, but it would suit me just fine: a four-seat, high-wing Cessna 172. My wife was a bit shaky about the prospect of us owning our own plane. It would mean I would be flying a lot more, with more opportunity for bad landings. I assured her that the Cessna 172 was the safest general aviation aircraft in the sky—the Volvo of small aircraft.

Part of the process of purchasing a plane is transferring all of the paperwork from seller to buyer. The Federal Aviation Administration (FAA) gives you only a month to get it done. Miss that deadline, and you're grounded. (I haven't changed the name of the agency in this story because there is only one organization in charge of registering aircraft.)

As soon as I'd taken possession of the airplane, I dutifully collected and filled out all of the necessary forms. One had to go to the Federal Communications Commission. Another went to the state of Oregon. The actual transfer of ownership was handled by the FAA itself.

The transfer of ownership paperwork includes a set of multipart paper forms, which are filled out by buyer and seller. It took the seller and me a couple of days to get together to sign the paperwork. Once all was complete, I stamped the envelope, and off it went to FAA headquarters in Wichita, Kansas.

I waited for the registration papers to arrive. I waited some more. I became nervous, but waited even a little longer after that; after all, I was dealing with the government. Each daily walk to the mailbox became a tension-filled trek, as I wondered whether I would get my registration back before the day I'd be grounded. Finally, just two days before the deadline, there it was: the return envelope from the FAA.

I opened it.

Dear Mr. Burley:

We have not been able to process your aircraft registration transfer, as we were not able to read the change of address on the registration form. If you could please resubmit the form with your address written more legibly, we will be able to complete the registration process. Thank you for your cooperation.

Sincerely,

Helen Phiser—Documents Processing Facility, FAA

The situation was absurd.

The letter was stating that my address, as written on the multipart form, was illegible. However, the notice telling me that my address was not legible had been sent to the very address that Ms. Phiser claimed she could not make out.

Standing on a country road in front of my mailbox, the letter in my hand, I guffawed in disbelief. Had anyone in the Documents Processing Facility of the FAA, I wondered, considered the irony of the letter the office had sent me? *Apparently not.*

My aircraft registration was about to expire because some Kansas bureaucrats had been breathing too much jet fuel.

I called the number listed on the letter and asked the operator to connect me with Ms. Phiser.

After a few minutes of recorded aviation-related warnings, Helen Phiser came on the line.

I explained the letter I had received, and jokingly asked, "Pretty funny, isn't it?"

"I don't see anything at all funny about it, Mr. Burley." She was serious. "We do our jobs here as well as we can. I don't know what we sent you, but if we said that your address was not legible, it wasn't."

"Then, how did you send me the letter to tell me that you couldn't read my address?" I replied.

"Mr. Burley, I don't have time to argue with you. You need to fill out the forms properly and return them to us, so that we can complete the transfer of registration. That is all I can tell you."

Following the events of 9/11, I wholly expected the FAA to have been transformed into a cracker-jack organization: professional, proficient, and precise. Clearly, it was as bogged-down in bureaucratic ineptitude as ever.

Something had to be done.

I had a pretty good idea of how to handle this, because I had already intuited something important about Ms. Phiser: she was a lifer.

"Ms. Phiser, as much as I appreciate that you have protocols you must follow, I am also aware that the FAA has been under some scrutiny lately for inefficiencies and delays in adopting new technologies."

Silence.

I had arrived at the appropriate place and time to create some "Trouble with a Capital T." It was time to make it personal.

"Although you may not find any humor in my situation, I'm sure you can see the inefficiency of it. I am also certain that if I were to share this story with certain members of the House Aviation Subcommittee, with your name prominently featured in the first paragraph of my letter, they might find this to be exactly the type of old-fashioned, blind-leading-the-blind thinking they've been talking about in regard to your agency. I see their point. I mean, really, why do we need people processing registration documents anyway? Couldn't your job be handled just as well by a secure online web form?"

She coughed.

"It's obvious that somewhere in your system, someone goofed. I didn't do anything wrong, so I shouldn't be the one having to resubmit forms and wait another two weeks while you do what you do to them.

"You have a choice to make right now. If you ask me again to fill out a new form and send it to you, I will. I will also send your letter and the original form to your boss and copies to each member of the Aviation Subcommittee of the U.S. House of Representatives, along with a full account of our conversation."

"I wish you wouldn't do that," Ms. Phiser said meekly.

"In that case, I think we should go with door number two. Let's acknowledge that I filled out the forms properly, and therefore you are able to complete the transfer of ownership. Given the late date, I would like to request that you send the document via overnight courier. Would that be possible?"

"I think we can still meet that deadline," replied Ms. Phiser. "But I will still need the completed transfer form."

"Which I will send to you in a day or so, agreed?"

"That will be fine," she said. "I'll make sure the registration goes out today. Just one more thing: I'll need to get your address."

THE ULTIMATE TECHNIQUE

The ultimate Unscrewed technique is…prevention.

No one ever chooses to do business with a company that is going to treat her badly, provide poor customer service, or rip her off. We walk into every situation bright-eyed and optimistic that we will be treated fairly and with respect. But that's not always the way things turn out, because we often miss warning signs that could save us from falling into the clutches of unprincipled companies or individuals.

We are programmed from birth to be consumers. We buy things, believing that there is a fixed set of rules that govern those transactions: we give them our money; they give us a product. If the product doesn't work, we believe we can ask them nicely to make things right, and they will happily cooperate. *We were programmed wrong.*

What you're not taught is that you have the economic leverage only as long as your money is still in your wallet. Until you hand that over, you are the one with the power. That is why the salesperson chases you around the store. It's why advertisers spend billions every year, trying to attract your attention. They want you to take your money out of your wallet and give it to them.

However, the moment the money changes hands—in the split second that you lay the bills on the counter—the balance of power swings in the direction of the company. Now, they have the money, and the power. If you want anything, you have to ask them for help, because in some fashion, even though you have purchased the product, it's still theirs. When it fails, they get to make the final decision: repair or replace. Even if they do replace it, they often send a "refurbished" item, rather than a new one.

On the other hand, they don't have to ask you for anything. You gave them money. Money doesn't ever "go bad." Money doesn't need spare parts, maintenance, or technical support. They won't ever need to get a refund on faulty currency. (Actually, if they ever did, you'd be in far more trouble than this book can help you with.)

Clearly, it's not a balanced relationship. You are still dependent on them; they need nothing more from you.

Also left out of our early consumer education is the concept that every business transaction is a negotiation. Sure, stores put price labels on all their items, and a new car wears an MSRP (Manufacturer's Suggested Retail Price) sticker when it's in the showroom window. Those are just asking prices. Most of us understand that the price of a car is negotiable. But have you ever thought to negotiate the cost of a set of tires, a new jacket, or a hotel room? You can always offer something else. Maybe they'll say no. Maybe they'll say yes. You can always ask for the terms of a contract to be modified. Maybe they'll say no. Often they'll say yes. You can always ask them to include the extended warranty as part of the purchase. Maybe they'll say no. Maybe they'll say yes. We have been indoctrinated to believe that negotiating the price in some situations is rude or tacky. Ask yourself who benefits from that belief. Certainly not consumers!

Take your time when making a purchase. Consider whether you need an item, whether you can afford it, whether it's offered in the right size or color or flavor, and so on. Also consider how you're feeling. Ask yourself the question, *What would make me feel really great about this purchase?* Then ask for it. All they can do is say no. But they don't want to. They want your money as much as—or more than—you want that new gadget, sofa, or dress. Every purchase is a hand of poker, whether you're looking across the cash register at the florist or sitting across the desk from the car sales manager.

The irony of our consumer society is that although most of us work very hard to earn our money, many of us do not give equal consideration to how we spend it. Getting the most bang for the buck starts out with a pair of tried-and-true axioms.

AXIOM NUMBER ONE:
IF IT LOOKS TOO GOOD TO BE TRUE, IT PROBABLY IS

Every so often I receive a call from some guy in a boiler room investment operation trying to pitch me on some new stock. My simple question to him always is, "If this is so great, why are you calling me—a stranger thousands of miles away—with this marvelous tip? Why are you on the phone with me with this great deal instead of your mother, father, aunt, uncle, brother, sister, or college roommate?" When an unbelievable deal appears, always ask yourself that question: *Why is this wonderful opportunity being offered to me?* Great deals do appear, but they are rare.

AXIOM NUMBER TWO:
THE LOWEST PRICE IS NOT ALWAYS THE BEST DEAL

Factory outlet stores are springing up like weeds alongside major freeways across the country. You may think that you can find the same merchandise you would find in a regular retail store, but at a substantial discount. This is not true. Much of the clothing and other merchandise found at factory outlets are seconds: damaged, returned, irregular, or display goods the manufacturers cannot sell as new. I'm not saying you can't get a good deal now and then at these places. Just be aware that you are not getting the same merchandise that you would at the mall. Plus, some companies are now manufacturing lower-quality merchandise for sale specifically at the outlet stores.

MAKING A GOOD INVESTMENT

There is no way to guarantee that all products you purchase will be high quality and low maintenance. However, there are several things you can do prior to your purchase that will greatly enhance your chances of making a good investment.

Know What You Are Buying

When you purchase a product or service from a company, you are also investing in a long-term partnership. The real price of the product is the sticker price, plus how much of your time will be needed to deal with problems during the lifespan of the product. A new cell phone is a $40 piece of aluminum and plastic with a $600 two-year contract attached. It could be a great deal if the phone works when and where you need it. But if the signal area doesn't cover your home, it's not such a great deal. Pay $300 for a new vacuum cleaner, and you are also buying into a five-year partnership of product quality and customer service with the manufacturer. That $300 is a great deal if the machine performs as expected. It's a lousy investment if it breaks down, even under warranty. If you value your free time at $100 per hour and you spend three hours dealing with a broken machine, it's now a $600 vacuum cleaner.

Do Some Research

Online consumer sites, such as the *Consumer Reports* web site, can be helpful. You can also get product reviews on many web sites, such as Amazon.com. For household products, mainstream magazines also do product reviews. Don't bother with "Buyers' Guide" publications (with the exception of the ones from *Consumer Reports*). Many of these have reviews that are paid for by the advertisers—skewing the results, wouldn't you think? After just a little research, you'll get a pretty good idea of the winners and the losers.

Use Your Radar

Pay attention to how you feel about the company and product from the first moment of contact with the salesperson, web site, or advertisement. In a store, a well-informed sales-person reflects a company that invests in training, so you are more likely to get what you need, rather than just the highest-priced item. When there's a problem, you are also more likely to get quick, accurate answers from a staff that is experienced in dealing with the manufacturers. If you are having problems during the purchasing process—getting your questions answered, finding someone to help you, or locating feature information on a web site—walk away. A company that provides poor service at the time of sale will not likely be a stellar provider of customer service when things go wrong.

Get References
Businesses ask for references all the time. Consumers should, too. For any purchase greater than $500, I ask for a couple names of people who have been there ahead of me. This is particularly important for small and local businesses. I've met the nicest owners who were the worst businesspeople. If they can't give you the names of three happy customers, run away. And some of the most helpful references can come from your friends. Just ask them.

Get the Legal Lowdown
Consumer protection agencies and the Better Business Bureau have a generally weak track record when it comes to preventing consumer abuse. However, it never hurts to check with them as part of an overall prevention effort. Do not rely solely on their reports (see chapter 1).

CONTROLLING YOUR ASSETS
Even when you take basic precautions during the buying process, it's much easier to stay Unscrewed if you keep tight control of your assets. Here are some basic rules.

Never Use Direct Draft
Never give any company the ability to draw funds directly from your checking account. Not your insurance company.

Not your mortgage company. Not your stockbroker. News-paper headlines scream every day about how personal infor-mation is stolen from company computers. If your credit card information is stolen, you can quickly cancel the card. If a crook snags your checking account information, all your money can be gone in an instant and the bank has no respon-sibility to cover your loss. The best you could hope for would be a financial settlement from the company that lost your data, though I wouldn't count on it. In February, 2006, a fed-eral appellate court ruled that companies aren't necessarily financially liable for losses you incur when they fail to protect your information.

Don't Pay by Cash or Check

When you pay with paper—either cash or a check—you are instantly handing your money to the company. You've kept 100 percent of your promise. There's no guarantee that the com-pany will keep its promise of a high-quality product or service. If there's a problem, you must depend on the company to live up to its part of the bargain. That's the basic problem: it is in the position of power, because it has your money. If the com-pany isn't nice about it, go into Unscrewed planning mode.

Pay by Credit Card

Most credit card companies require merchants to have a thirty-day money-back guarantee. The merchants don't usu-ally tell you about it. Sometimes they'll claim the thirty-day guarantee as their own, but it's really part of their agreement with the bank. Even past the thirty-day return, many credit cards will protect you from manufacturer's defects for a full year. This protection doesn't cost you a thing…as long as you pay off your cards every month. But, of course, the credit card companies are counting on you *not* to do that.

If you pay attention to the ten prepurchase recommenda-tions in this chapter, the number of times you get screwed will go way down. Just ask yourself a few questions, put a finger in the air to see which way the wind is blowing, and take a big sniff to see whether the deal smells like roses or rotten eggs. Above all, don't let the advertising-induced "gotta have it right now" feeling take over. If you don't feel right about it, walk away.

* * *

As you'll read in the following trio of stories, some companies have figured out how to provide great products and great customer service at the same time.

UNSCREWED TRUE STORIES
Perfect Customer Service

Throughout most of this book, I've given examples of poor customer service, ridiculous employee statements, and downright stupid corporate policies. However, as I've also pointed out, nine out of ten companies still make a good attempt at keeping their customers happy.

I'm going to share with you three stellar examples of customer service. The names have not been changed, so that I can give credit where credit is due. I have no financial interest in these companies. I am sharing their stories only as a primer for the rest of the corporate community in how to create and retain happy customers.

The Coffee Giant
Many residents of the Pacific Northwest suffer from an addiction: caffeine. Espresso consumption is nearly a religion in these parts. The sect has spread to other parts of the country, but it is at its most aromatic in the Pacific Northwest: the home of Starbucks.

My wife and I purchase both Starbucks coffee and Starbucks products. So far, we have an espresso machine, a bean grinder, coffee storage bins, and a drip coffeemaker.

One morning not too long ago, I carefully ground a half-caff mixture of Colombian Supremo, put precisely twelve scoops into our Starbucks coffeemaker, pushed the brew button…and nothing happened.

I made sure that it was plugged in, that the outlet worked, and that everything was set up correctly. After running through the checklist a couple of times, I could only conclude that the $150 Starbucks Barista Aroma Grande coffeemaker was on the fritz.

I logged onto the Starbucks Internet site and located the customer service number. I knew I'd be playing from a position of weakness from the start, as I had purchased the coffeemaker many months earlier at one of the seven Starbucks outlets in our town, but I couldn't remember which one. I searched my receipt box and couldn't find one for the coffeemaker. I couldn't even remember which credit card I had used to pay for it.

I dialed the toll-free number, which was answered instantly by a young man who introduced himself as Joseph.

"How can I make your day better?" he asked.

"You can tell me where I send my coffeemaker to be repaired."

"Is it one of ours?"

"Yes, a Barista Aroma Grande. I've had it for about a year. This morning, it just decided to stop working."

"Are you near one of our stores?"

"Yes, I'm in Eugene. I bought it at one of them, though I honestly can't remember which one."

"That doesn't matter," Joseph said. "Would you mind holding for one minute?"

"That would be fine," I replied, though I wondered why he didn't just give me the Repair Center address and get me off the line.

Joseph interrupted Sheryl Crow about a minute later.

"I called the store at Eighteenth and Pearl Streets, and it has a Barista Aroma Grande in stock. Do you know where that store is?"

"Yes."

"If you take your machine down there, they will be happy to exchange it."

"But I don't have a receipt."

"No problem. We know that you must have purchased it from us somewhere. Is that going to work for you?"

"Yes, great. I can be there in a half hour."

"Would you mind holding for one more moment, please? I'll be right back."

"I'll be here." Sheryl Crow had segued into a new cut from Green Day. I heard only a few bars before Joseph came back on the line.

"I spoke with Alan at our store. He'll be expecting you."

I was astounded. Sans receipt, on my word alone, this young customer service representative had twice called a local store to arrange an appointment for me to exchange my broken coffeemaker.

"Thank you, Joseph. You are an excellent representative of your company. I hope you'll go far."

"Thank you. Glad I could help you out. Have a great day."

That phone call was the closest I've come to the perfect customer service experience. I felt completely respected as a customer. My problem was solved almost instantly, and the company representative had gone out of his way to make sure that the arrangements would be convenient. By the way, when I dropped the defunct coffeemaker off at the store, Alan apologized for the problem. And he tossed in an extra thermal carafe.

* * *

What Starbucks did right was assume that I was telling the truth. The representative never questioned whether I had somehow damaged the coffeemaker. If I had, what difference would it have made? The company might have saved $40 in profit on a refund, but do you think that I would have returned to Starbucks to purchase my next caffeine creation machine?

Unlike many of the companies I've talked about—with adversarial, cost-reduction-oriented Customer Service Departments—Starbucks management sees customer service as a sales opportunity, a chance to win over a customer for life. This philosophy appears at all levels. If they get your order wrong, they not only fix you a new drink, but very often give you a coupon for a free beverage for the next time, just because you had to wait a few extra minutes while they corrected the problem. They never say, "That's not what you said." Even if it were true, what would they have to gain? A dollar profit on that drink? Instead, by sticking to the old maxim, "The customer is always right," they build a loyal customer base that seeks them out for quality of product and experience.

The Electronics Giant

I'm always the first on the block to get the latest electronic gadget. So, a few years ago, when high-definition television first arrived on the scene, I had to have one right away—even if only two channels of HD programming were available at the time.

My son and I drove to the local Circuit City store and spent an hour perusing, measuring, adjusting, and annoying…until I decided on one of the units with a forty-eight-inch screen. It was kind of pricey, more than $3,000, but it was beautiful.

I couldn't exactly fit the unit into the trunk of my sports car, so I arranged for delivery. Amazingly, they were able to drop off the new set the very next day. Two strong young fellows carried the set into our family room, assembled the stand, mounted the new TV, and made sure the connections worked properly. They even took their shoes off every time they entered and exited the house.

That night, the entire family sat down to watch our new high-definition television. My wife and kids thought it was fantastic. Regrettably, I was underwhelmed. On the upper right corner of the screen, I could see a little square that stayed red all the time, even when the rest of the picture went black. It was just one tiny little pixel. My wife couldn't even see it, but I knew it was there.

I wondered whether there was some way to reset it, so I called the manufacturer's Customer Service line. After winding my way through the voice mail maze, I was finally able to speak with a television technician.

"Just one pixel?" he asked.

"Yes."

"That's within tolerances. Manufacturing specifications say there should be no more than four stagnant pixels before the set is rejected."

"But it looks terrible," I said. "I just got it yesterday, and I'm already regretting my purchase."

"I'm sorry," said the tech. "That's our policy."

Of course, I was fuming. I started to put together my Unscrewed Plan to take care of this technological indecency. But before I fired both barrels back at the manufacturer, I thought I'd check in with the Circuit City store, too.

A single-level voice mail system connected me directly with the Television Department at the store where I had purchased my new set. I explained the situation. "No problem," said the salesperson. "That may be their policy, but it's not ours. We've got a thirty-day 'no questions asked' return policy. I'll have a new one out to your house—let me check—will tomorrow work for you?"

"Sure," I said, surprised they were willing to deliver on a Saturday.

At nine the next morning, the same two guys who had brought the original TV showed up with a new one. In less than ten minutes, they'd hauled away the original TV and installed the replacement set. Before they left, they made sure that we turned it on and perused all the pixels.

"Every last one is black, red, green, or blue," I said, very pleased. "Thanks so much for the quick service."

"No problem," they said in unison.

The new set worked perfectly. However, after a couple of months, I started to notice red fringing around the sides of the picture. I supposed that it had always been there, but I only noticed it at certain times, mostly while watching programs that had a lot of white backgrounds. It was very annoying, so I called the manufacturer's Customer Service line again.

"It's a known problem," said the technician.

"What do you mean?" I asked. "You mean that you make sets you know are faulty?"

"It's just the nature of the projection system we're using. It creates a chromatic aberration when the reflective main mirror…blah, blah, blah." All he was telling me was that I'd be stuck with red fringes because they didn't have a design team that knew how to make a TV set without them.

I wasn't sure that the guy was telling the truth, so I decided to check with "my boys" at the Circuit City store. It wasn't even their responsibility anymore. I was well beyond the thirty-day "no questions asked" return policy.

Circuit City's Television Department picked up the phone on the second ring. I told the guy my story. Turned out that he was the salesperson, Vince, who had sold me the original set.

"Didn't we replace that once for you already?" he asked.

I wasn't sure I liked the direction this was headed.

"Yes, but I'm just calling to see whether you've heard of this particular problem before. I'm not asking for you to take it back or anything."

"Why not? Doesn't seem like this is *your* fault. Sounds to me like a manufacturing defect."

I was speechless.

"Mr. Burley, why don't you come down to the store?" Vince asked. "You can take a look at some of the other sets.

We can talk, and I hope that we can find one that won't give you so much trouble. If it's convenient, I'll be here until five today."

"I can be there in about an hour," I replied.

Vince walked the Circuit City aisles with me for almost an hour, until I decided on a new set, from a different company. The price was a few hundred dollars more, but I felt certain I would finally be happy with it. I offered Vince my credit card.

"Not going to need that," he said. "After all the trouble you've been through, I'm going to discount the new one. Just want to make sure you get something that will make you happy. All right with you?"

All right with me? I was probably a little too boisterous in my gratitude, though I stopped short of hugging him. It wasn't that I was so happy to get a new television set. I was really just amazed that there was a company that would allow its employees so much leeway to keep their customers happy. I had given up hope that quality big-box customer service could still be found between the Right and Left Coasts.

* * *

While I was in college, I actually worked for a big-box electronic retailer, whose philosophy was about as far away from Circuit City's as could be imagined. We used to offer our customers salted popcorn and champagne on the way into the store, and would get bonus points from the management if a customer was forced to run out to the car for change to pay the last dollar or so on the bill. I don't remember that store ever taking an item back. It went out of business years ago.

Circuit City's handling of my situation with the television was about the most extraordinary example of customer service I've ever seen from a product retailer.

I have learned since that the company will take anything back, without question, within that thirty-day period…and, obviously, sometimes beyond. Its view of customer service is similar to that of Starbucks: Never give a customer a reason to go anywhere else. Rather than seeing me as a problem customer who was just too picky, the salespeople treated me as a loyal customer who had yet to be fully satisfied. If they had handled it differently, they might have kept the profit on the first sale, maybe $1,000. But since that incident, I've spent more than $10,000 at Circuit City, generating even greater profits for them.

The Little Giant

Giving someone a new coffeemaker without even a receipt is impressive customer service. Trading in television sets and changing policies for a finicky customer is also notable. But what would you think of a company that lets you take a product, beat the hell out of it for six months, and then return it—just because you didn't really need it?

About ten years ago, we moved onto farm acreage in Oregon. My wife and I were both city kids, so we really didn't know what we were getting into. The property had been pretty much abandoned for two years before we bought it. The blackberry bushes, thistles, and field grass looked as though they were going to devour the house, garage, and quarter-mile driveway. We figured that we needed some heavy equipment to take care of this botanical wasteland.

After checking all the catalogs and online sites, and watching endless hours of Home & Garden TV, we were convinced that we needed a field and brush mower.

For the rurally uneducated, the Country Home Products Field and Brush Mower looks like a rotary lawn mower on steroids. It is a self-propelled, walk-behind machine capable of cutting down saplings as large as two and one-half inches thick. Looking out upon our version of a Panamanian rain forest transplanted to Oregon, we decided that we needed the most powerful machine we could get.

We ordered the mower online, and it arrived by truck less than a week later. Following simple assembly instructions, I had the unit up and running in about two hours.

For the next several weeks, I drove that mower up and down our hillsides, clearing creeks, paths, and meadows. After a month, I had obliterated every errant wild weed and thicket I could find. It soon became clear that after that major grooming, we'd never need the big mower again: a simple string trimmer would take care of the maintenance.

The mower had cost us almost $3,000. That was when Hali mentioned the "six-month, risk-free trial period" that had been advertised on the web site when we bought the machine.

I looked at the mower. It was pretty beat up. I mean, I wasn't very experienced in using heavy equipment, so I'd driven it into a few creeks and gullies. It was caked with mud and dented. I thought, *There is no way in the world that they will still take this back.*

"It's worth a try," Hali said.

Completely expecting a well-deserved rejection, I called the Country Home Products Customer Service line. I was totally honest with them about the unit. "I used it and it worked great," I said. "It's just too much mower for our property."

"That's no problem," said Mary, the customer helper (that's what she called herself).

"I have to be honest," I told her. "It's not in the best condition. I took care of the oil and everything, but it has seen some use. I may have run it into a ditch or two while I was getting the hang of it."

"We place no conditions on the six-month trial. You will get a full refund. I've got your information. A truck will be by to pick up the unit sometime in the next several days. The driver will call first to make sure that you'll be there."

I still couldn't believe the company would take the machine back for a full refund, sight unseen. "Are you going to need a credit card for the shipping charges?" I asked.

"No. That's taken care of, Mr. Burley. I'm sorry the mower didn't fit your needs. I hope that you will consider us in the future."

"Thank you. I will." And I meant it. A year later, we purchased a smaller unit, more appropriate for our needs. Since then, we've upgraded that machine and recommended the company to dozens of our neighbors. And now, I recommend Country Home Products to you. (I'm telling you, a company can't *buy* this kind of advertising!)

* * *

What do these three retailers' customer service policies have in common? The companies look far beyond the immediate transaction, making the assumption that if they create a loyal customer, they will recoup the immediate loss several times over in the long run.

This kind of long view is rare in business these days: many companies are driven by short-term stock values and quarterly sales revenues. But these three retailers—Starbucks, Circuit City, and Country Home Products—have learned that, in the end, sophisticated consumers "buy the company" as well as the product.

THE UNSCREWED TRUTH

In previous chapters, I've written about what has happened to customer service, why it's happened, and how we have been affected. I've avoided pointing the finger of blame—until now. The question of who is responsible for the crisis of customer versus company has a simple answer. After years of research, I have concluded that the ultimate villain is looking back at you—and me—in the mirror.

"But I've never screwed anybody out of anything!" you protest. That's possibly true. Nevertheless, to the extent that we all participate in, and exalt, our current economic system of capitalism without conscience, we are all responsible for the accelerating erosion of customer service and product quality.

Our economic system fosters a predatory environment that pits customer against company in a battle for the contents of your wallet. Economic success is based on profit. Any student in Economics 101 can tell you that profit is the difference between what a product or service costs the company to produce and sell, and what it is sold for to the customer. The goal for companies within our capitalist economic system is to maximize profit. In other words, a company's primary objective is to convince the customer to pay as much as possible for something while the company minimizes its cost, or real value.

Therefore, we have a system where the most successful company of all would have a product that is perceived to have infinite value while, in fact, having minimal real value.

Just as we root for the outnumbered Jedi as they battle the dark forces of the Empire, so, too, do we root for such companies as Starbucks, Circuit City, and Country Home Products to set an example of product quality and customer service that spreads across the globe. (Just as easily, they could each fall victim to a ruthlessly aggressive competitor offering the illusion of quality, instead of the reality.)

As global competition increases, profit margins—the difference between the cost to the company and the price paid by the customer—will be squeezed. Margins can be expanded in only two ways: 1) increase what a customer is willing to pay and 2) decrease the cost of production.

Clever marketing campaigns can push prices up only so far before customers stop buying. The only other option to maintain margins is to cut the cost of production, which is not limited to the actual manufacturing aspects of a business. The cost of production includes all the other expenses related to running the enterprise, including salaries, advertising, rent, phone lines, and customer support.

Megaretailer Wal-Mart has taken a lot of flak for aggressive, and occasionally predatory, business practices. The unfortunate truth is that Wal-Mart is the inevitable end result of the profit-at-all-cost retail system we have created, fostered, and promoted to the rest of the world. Wal-Mart is the great white shark of economic evolution: a perfectly formed corporate predator.

Wal-Mart can provide the lowest-priced items because it has uncompromisingly controlled its cost of production. The company is infamous for hard-ball negotiating tactics with suppliers, who can then provide only the bare minimum needed to fulfill the contract.

If you buy a yellow T-shirt for $8 from Wal-Mart, it may look like any other yellow T-shirt, except that you can be sure it was made with the lowest-cost materials, by the cheapest labor. The end result is a product that appears to have high value, but is really of low value. The cloth will wear out. The thread will give way. The color will fade. Is an $8 T-shirt that lasts three months a better deal than a $12 T-shirt that lasts a year? Of course not.

Wal-Mart is not the only company playing this game. It is only the most successful. Designer jeans are not intrinsically more valuable than off-brand jeans. We buy cheap jeans at high prices because we are taught to value the label more than the product itself. Assuming they are made of the same materials with the same techniques, their real value is the same. Advertisers convince us that the designer products are more valuable by creating an illusion of increased value where none really exists. What is the real value of a name stamped on a label? What messages are we responding to? Can companies really justify the $50 difference between two pairs of identical double-stitched jeans?

We must stop paying attention to what advertisers tell us, and instead make our buying decisions based on the real long-term value of a product, which includes the ability of the company to give us customer service and our own future cost in time and money spent dealing with customer service representatives.

How are we supposed to measure real value? Most of us have such harried lives that we can't always take the time to do much research or comparison shopping. Even if we could, how can we make truly informed decisions about the quality versus price of two similar products? We can't.

For the transformation to occur, the system must change. And for that to happen, legions of us will have to decide that we are going to pay only for real value and stop paying for imaginary value. The pair of double-stitched blue jeans will not increase in value just because it has a designer's name on it, unless that company has demonstrated the product to be of genuinely higher quality. We will need proof that the $8 Wal-Mart T-shirt is equivalent to its $12 counterpart before we blindly decide we're getting a better deal from the megastore.

Only when that happens will corporations be compelled to provide quality products and services at reasonable prices, and to stand behind those products by providing real customer service, thereby making good on the initial contract: value provided for money paid.

Given this change in perceptions, we can create a society in which companies are expected to be more than just profit-and-loss entities. When we begin to think of our consumer-selves as equal partners with the corporations, and demand a return to the concept of corporate citizenship, companies will become institutions that participate in our communities at many levels, and they will measure their success as much by the satisfaction of their customers as by their own bottom line.

UNSCREWED TRUE STORY
Sometimes They Make It Easy

I've never figured out why banks charge $35 for a bounced check. In these days of computerized transactions, it can't really cost them more than a few cents to figure out that there aren't enough funds in the account. Even if you count the cost of an envelope and stamp to send it back, the total cost can't be more than a few dollars. So why is there such an astronomical fee? Are they profiting from someone's mistake? That doesn't seem right. Perhaps it's a penalty. But if you bounce a check for $5, it's a 700 percent fine. So it's profit or penalty, and I don't particularly like the smell of either option. Bounced-check charges always hurt the people who can least afford to pay them. (Something has to be done, but that's a topic for a future book.)

Anyway, a while ago, my friends Randy and Kate called me about some bounced checks.

Kate had been with her bank, Western Territorial, for several years and—to be entirely honest—once in a while lost track of her account and bounced some checks. Knowing that it was her fault, she dutifully paid the fees, which often compounded into several hundred dollars after the checks were resubmitted and bounced again and again. The obvious solution would have been overdraft protection. However, Kate and her husband were both schoolteachers with normal levels of credit card debt and a home mortgage. Ironically, it was the history of bounced checks that put them below the credit score where she would have qualified for overdraft protection.

One Monday morning, Kate's debit card didn't work at the gas station. She thought something might be wrong with the card, so she called the bank and got the manager, Jeff, on the phone. He told her that her account was $8 short as of that morning, causing three checks to bounce. Charges on the checks pushed her negative balance to $113 in the red. (Of course, the bank hadn't paid the checks. That way, they could bounce again and incur even more charges.)

"That's impossible," Kate said. "I should have more than $100 in my account."

"That's not what our records show," Jeff answered.

"That's got to be wrong. I'm sure of it," Kate pleaded. "This time, I've been writing everything down."

Given her history, Kate could almost hear Manager Jeff thinking, *I've heard that one before.*

Instead, he replied, "I don't know what to tell you, except that you probably should get some money into the account right away, so that no more checks bounce."

Kate was positive that she should have more than $100 left in her account, but she began to doubt herself. "I'll be right down," she said, also knowing that her husband wouldn't be happy that he'd have to bail her out again. His name wasn't even on the account.

Randy wrote her a check from their 401k retirement account to cover the overdrafts. She drove down to the Western Territorial branch and deposited it at the teller window, just to make sure it was credited that afternoon. At the last minute, she thought to ask the woman at the Customer Service desk, Frannie, whether she could get a printout of her most recent transactions. In a minute, she had it in her hand, and saw the problem.

"Frannie, I bought a planter at Jack's Garden Shop for $150 on Saturday. I used my debit card. When I got it home, it didn't fit where I thought it would, so I took it back. It was the same day. The store gave me a credit. I see the charge, but the credit isn't on here."

"That's not our area," Frannie said. "You'll have to check with the store."

Kate dug through her purse. "But I've got the refund receipt right here."

"I'm sorry," said Frannie, comparing the account record with the refund slip. "I can see they gave you the credit, but it's not on your account, so I don't think they actually processed it."

Kate was furious. She went immediately to the garden shop.

She charged up to the cash register, waving the refund slip and bank record.

"You guys have cost me more than $100 in bounced-check fees because you didn't give me my credit on the planter."

The owner, Jack, appeared over her shoulder.

"Hi, Kate," he said calmly. "Look, if this is our fault, I'll take care of it. Don't worry. You're a good customer."

Jack asked her to follow him to his office in the back. Kate waited as he scanned the register tapes from the weekend.

Jack held up the master printout that had been sent to the bank. "I don't know what to tell you, Kate. Both transactions are here. Here's your purchase. Here's the credit. And here's the printout from the batch we transmitted to Western Territorial, showing both. It's our bank, too, so the transactions should have cleared right away."

Kate was at a loss: the bank said that it was the store's fault, but the store records clearly showed the canceled purchase and the refund. Unsure of what to do, she went home. When Randy got home that night, she told him the story. He was as puzzled as she was, but was sure of one thing: it wasn't her fault. Blame belonged either to the store or to the bank. There was no way she should have to pay those fees.

Something had to be done.

"Honey, let me take care of this. I'll give the manager a call in the morning." Kate didn't like always having to count on Randy to bail her out, but he had a way with such things.

The next morning, Randy called the branch. He got Manager Jeff on the phone.

"I know you spoke with my wife yesterday about this, but we've discovered some more information, and I'm sure that it's not her fault." Randy related what they'd found out about the debit and credit receipts from the garden shop.

"You're right. It's not her problem. It's the store's problem," Jeff said. "But not because they made a mistake. They just didn't understand the terms of their merchant account with regard to debit card credits."

"What do you mean?"

"Well, when you make a purchase with a debit card, the funds are removed from your account immediately," Jeff explained. "When a credit is issued on a debit card, it doesn't clear the bank until the end of the next full business day."

"Why is that?"

"It's just the way the system works."

"Then, it's the bank that really caused the problem here," Randy said. "You take the money out immediately, but take your sweet time about putting it back."

"I'm sorry, but that's the policy on debit refunds."

"If that's supposed to be an explanation, it isn't good enough," Randy said. "Your policy just cost my family more than $100, significant domestic tension, and considerable time while we tracked this down."

"I don't set bank policy."

"I don't care *who* sets the policy: it isn't right," Randy continued, feeling himself getting red-faced. "You're a pretty big bank. I suppose you could be floating a million dollars in refund credits every day. At the end of a year, that's some major interest in your pocket."

"Look," Jeff said, "I don't need to listen to your tirade."

"No, you don't," Randy said. "You *need* to put that money back into my wife's account by three this afternoon. If you don't, my next call will be to a reporter friend. I'll bet that he'll be interested in how you're taking advantage of working people, earning interest on delayed refunds, and charging outrageous fees after your policy has caused an overdraft. It's criminal!"

"I'm going to have to end this conversation now," said the bank manager.

The phone went dead before Randy could answer.

Randy wasn't sure whether he'd fixed things or not. *Guess I'll find out by three*, he thought.

He didn't have to wait that long. Just after noon, Kate called.

"They've canceled my account," she said. "Something about what you said to the branch manager."

Randy called the branch and asked to speak with Jeff. "He's out to lunch," he was told. He called back. "He's in a meeting," said another voice. Clearly, Jeff was ducking his calls. That was when Randy called me.

When he finished with the story, I said, "Randy, tell Kate that her account will be restored today, all fees will be refunded, she will receive a letter of apology from the bank, and the bank will gladly provide her the overdraft protection it has previously denied her."

Randy laughed. "Sounding mighty confident, aren't you?"

"This is an easy one," I said. "They made one mistake that is unforgivable."

I researched the bank online, and found the numbers for the Executive Offices. A perky receptionist answered. I asked to speak with the bank's corporate counsel.

I was connected to Corporate Counsel, and a voice said, "Teresa Hoyle."

"Ms. Hoyle," I said. "I'm calling on behalf of a friend who is having a small problem at a branch. May I ask just a minute of your time? I really think you should know about this."

"Go ahead," she said. I assumed she was timing me.

I gave her Kate's story; then I told Randy's side. "The next thing that happened was that the branch manager closed Kate's account, telling her it was because of something her husband had said."

"Is this a joint account?" she asked.

"No," I said. "Only Kate's name is on the account."

"Oh no." She sounded stunned.

"Yes, Ms. Hoyle," I continued mildly. "I see at least four errors in judgment here. First, a woman's bank account was closed because of something her husband—not a signatory on the account—told a branch manager. Second, that could be a violation of her civil rights. Third, it's certainly a violation of bank policy, if not federal law. Fourth, we've still got the question of why the bank floats the debit card credits a full business day."

Ms. Hoyle sighed. "Can I call you back in a few minutes?"

"You don't need to call me back," I said. "Check out the story. It's accurate, and here's what you need to do."

I talked with Randy and Kate that night. My predictions had all come true. Manager Jeff had even called Kate with an apology. In the end, though, after all that had happened, Kate decided she was going to close the account and take her business elsewhere. "Probably a good idea," I said.

* * *

I love the story of Randy and Kate. It's proof that once in a while you might be screwed in such an obvious way that the Unscrewing is almost effortless, even amusing.

And there is a second, *secret* Unscrewed Truth in Randy and Kate's story and in *every* screwed-up circumstance.

Somewhere in his or her greed, ineptitude, and hubris, every adversary has made an error in judgment that you can exploit to Unscrew the situation. You just need to find it.

And don't forget that you have a powerful, invisible advantage: you've read this book.

INDEX